289934

Messerschmitt Bf 109G-6/R2Trop, 6./JG 3 "Udet", home defence Germany 1944. Standard splinter upper surfaces, pale blue grey and green mottled fuselage sides. Yellow 6 and bar outlined black. Black and white striped spinner.

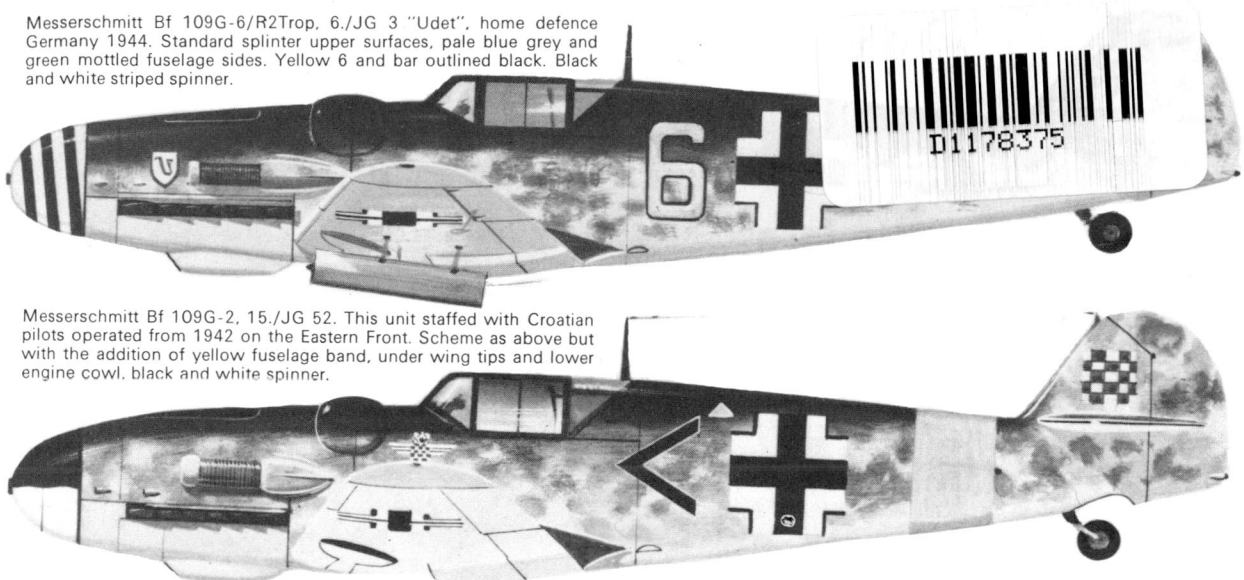

Messerschmitt Bf 109G-2, 15./JG 52. This unit staffed with Croatian pilots operated from 1942 on the Eastern Front. Scheme as above but with the addition of yellow fuselage band, under wing tips and lower engine cowl, black and white spinner.

MESSERSCHMITT Bf109 F-G
IN LUFTWAFFE & FOREIGN SERVICE

Text by Francis K. Mason

Illustrated and compiled by Richard Ward

ACKNOWLEDGEMENTS

This, the second volume in a series of four on the Messerschmitt Bf 109 covers the F and G models, the third volume will cover these two sub-types in greater photographic detail. Thanks are due, as always, to Herr Karl Reis Jr., and to all those who assisted with photographs and information whose names are listed below in alphabetical order:

G. Cattaneo, Borje Hielm, Italian AF, IWM, Mousescu Mihail, Hans Obert, Hans Redemann, Eino Ritaranta, Christopher F. Shores, Zdenek Titz, T. M. Thoronsen, USAF, Martin C. Windrow.

Bf 109G-14, Avia C-10 of the Czechoslovak Air Police. Overall grey with red nose, wing and tailplane leading edges and tips. Red registration outlined white.

Bf 109G-12, Avia C-110 two-seat trainer in overall silver scheme, black code.

Published by: Osprey Publishing Limited, England
Editorial Office: P.O. Box 5, Canterbury, Kent, England
Subscription & Business Office: P.O. Box 25, 707 Oxford Road, Reading, Berkshire, England
The Berkshire Printing Co. Ltd. © Osprey Publishing Ltd. 1973 ISBN 0 85045 153 1

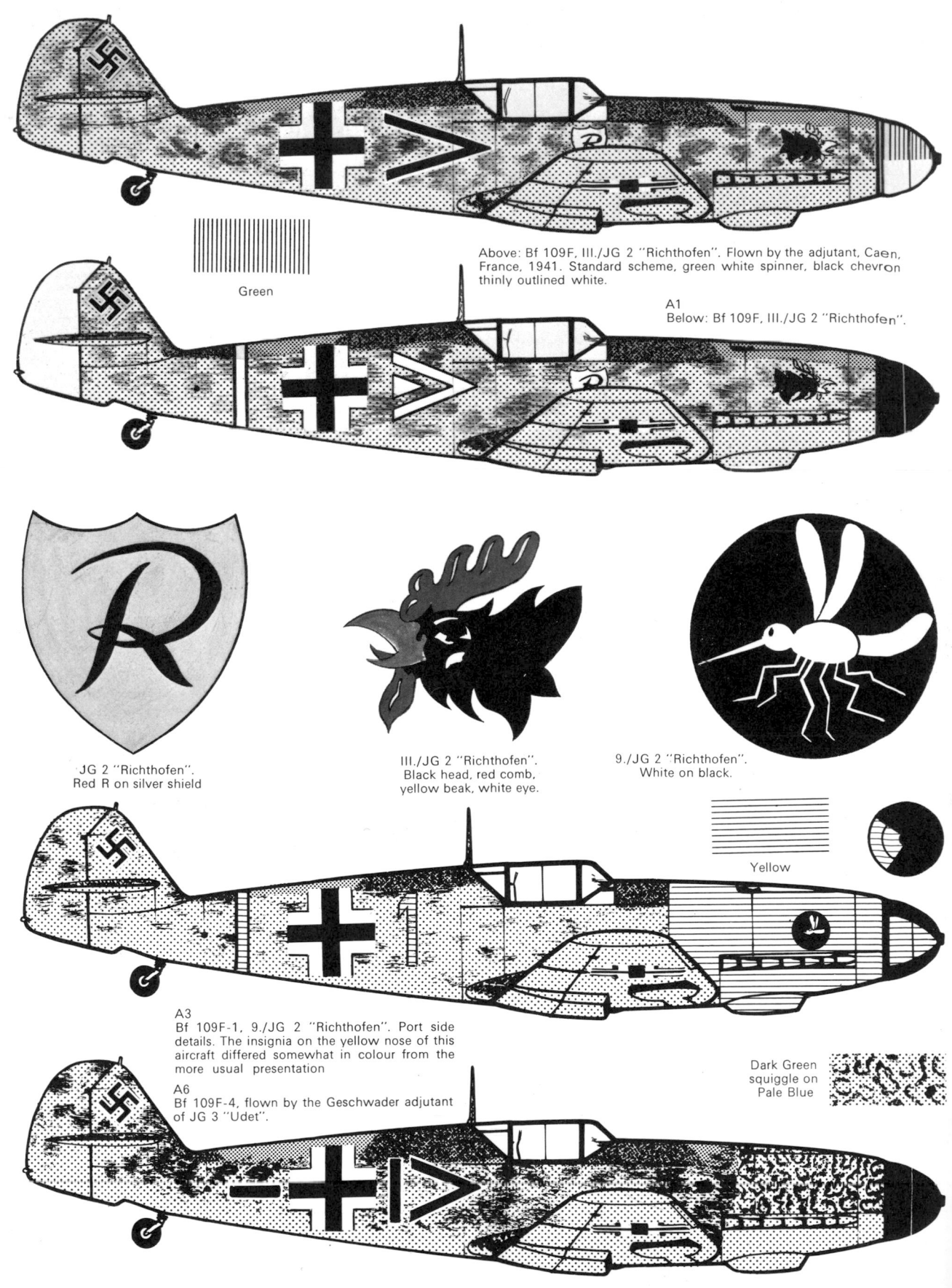

Green

Above: Bf 109F, III./JG 2 "Richthofen". Flown by the adjutant, Caen, France, 1941. Standard scheme, green white spinner, black chevron thinly outlined white.

A1
Below: Bf 109F, III./JG 2 "Richthofen".

JG 2 "Richthofen".
Red R on silver shield

III./JG 2 "Richthofen".
Black head, red comb,
yellow beak, white eye.

9./JG 2 "Richthofen".
White on black.

Yellow

A3
Bf 109F-1, 9./JG 2 "Richthofen". Port side details. The insignia on the yellow nose of this aircraft differed somewhat in colour from the more usual presentation

Dark Green squiggle on Pale Blue

A6
Bf 109F-4, flown by the Geschwader adjutant of JG 3 "Udet".

A Messerschmitt Bf 109G-2 of II./JG 54 "Grunherz" taxiing out for take-off on an airfield in Russia. Note the wheel covers have been removed. Black 1 and bar thinly outlined white, green heart outlined white and II Gruppe insignia ahead of cockpit. Yellow under cowl, fuselage band and wing tips, the fuselage has been painted in irregular bands of black green on dark green, upper surfaces standard splinter camouflage. A narrower yellow band is faintly visible through the green overpainting on the aft fuselage. (via T. M. Thoronsen)

MESSERSCHMITT Bf 109F/G

Although Professor Willy Messerschmitt's Bf 109E had spearheaded the *Luftwaffe*'s triumphant drive over Europe during 1939 and 1940, and borne the brunt of the daylight air combats over Britain during that fateful summer of 1940, the excellent fighter was by the spring of 1941 unquestionably inferior in Northern Europe to the Spitfire V—which commenced delivery to No. 92 Squadron, RAF, in March that year. Nevertheless the "Emil" continued to give unrivalled service for many months in North Africa prior to the appearance of later Spitfires in that theatre.

Such an eventual eclipse had been foreshadowed much earlier, and long before the Battle of Britain had reached its climax the next basic version of the Bf 109 made its first flight. On 10 July 1940 an "Emil" (*Werke Nr.* 5604) first flew with a 1,200 h.p. Daimler-Benz DB 601E-1 at Augsburg-Haunstetten. Still featuring the square-cut wingtips of the Bf 109E, this prototype (coded *VK+AB*) nevertheless featured considerable "cleaning-up" of the nose and eliminated the strut-braced tailplane in favour of a cantilever unit. As such it foreshadowed the most attractive of all variants—the Bf 109F.

Two further prototypes, the Bf 109V17 and V18, were built, these aircraft employing a new wing featuring extended, rounded tips and Frise-type ailerons and plain, unslotted flaps. Also introduced were a smaller rudder and retractable tailwheel. These aircraft were followed by a small pre-production batch of Bf 109F-Os which, as an interim measure, were powered by DB 601N engines (using flat-topped pistons and 100-octane fuel). The F-Os and initial production F-1s retained an armament of a hub-firing MG FF 20-mm. cannon and two nose-mounted synchronised MG 17 7.92-mm. machine-guns.

These early aircraft were delivered to Rechlin and other evaluation establishments in January 1941, only straightway to suffer a number of fatal accidents—unexplained until it was deduced that at certain engine speeds a sympathetic oscillation in the new tail unit was causing fracture of the tailplane spars and a consequent loss of the tail. All Bf 109Fs were returned to the factories for remedial action.

By the time the strengthened Bf 109F-1s reached frontline *Jagdgeschwader* early in March 1941 (at the same time that the Spitfire V was joining No 92 Squadron), the next sub-variant—the F-2—was already emerging from the factories. This featured a hub-firing MG 151 15-mm. cannon with a rate of fire of 950 rounds per minute, in addition to the customary nose-mounted MG 17s. This version was also tropicalised for service in North Africa (and was later used in South Russia). The Bf 109F-2/Z was a "sprint" version with GM-1 nitrous-oxide injection to provide short bursts of extra power above the engine's normal rated altitude.

The Bf 109F-1 and F-2 served throughout 1941 and were joined early in 1942 by the F-3 which was powered by the DB 601E using 87-octane B2 fuel. Retaining the F-2s armament, it had a top speed of 390 m.p.h. at 22,000 feet, a normal range of 440 miles and a service ceiling of 37,000 feet. Its initial rate of climb of 3,320 feet/minute was superior by a small margin to that of the Spitfire V but rather less than that of the Spitfire IX (which joined RAF Fighter Command in July 1942).

Strongly-held, yet sharply-divided views were expressed among the *Jagdflieger* concerning the merits of the hub-firing and nose-mounted guns (as they had been ever since the introduction of the "Emil"). While the opinions of such respected advocates of those nose guns as Werner Mölders were never treated lightly, it must be stated that the relatively slow, interrupted fire by synchronised guns together with engine-mounted cannon whose cooling was always open to doubt, scarcely amounted to a formidable gun armament—a view expressed by Adolf Galland. Thus the Bf 109F-4 was also introduced early in 1942, featuring a re-barrelled MG 151 in the hub-firing location, firing 20-mm. ammunition, but at the reduced rate of 650 rounds per minute. An alternative sub-variant, the Bf 109F-4/R-1, provided for an alternative installation of two 20-mm. MG 151s in bulky underwing gun packs. While perhaps adequate in hitting-power against Allied bombers of 1942, the Bf 109F's efficient aerodynamic lines were thus sullied by excrescences that badly detracted from its performance and rendered it markedly inferior to the contemporary Spitfire, and the progressive addition of such appendages henceforth marked the gradual decline of this otherwise truly beautiful version as an intercepting dogfighter.

Three other sub-variants of the Bf 109F were the F-4/B, equipped as a fighter-bomber capable of carrying either a single 500-kilo bomb or four 100-kilo bombs; the F-5, introduced in 1942 as a long-range reconnaissance fighter with armament reduced to the two MG 17 machine-guns and provision for a belly-mounted 66-Imp. gal. drop tank; and the F-6, also introduced in 1942 as a pure reconnaissance version with all armament removed and provision for the fuselage installation of either RB 20/30, RB 50/30 or RB 75/30 reconnaissance cameras mounted in the radio bay.

The Bf 109F in service

The Bf 109F entered *Luftwaffe* service early in 1941 and was almost extinct two years later. First to receive the F-2 was the *Geschwader Stab* and *III Gruppe* of *JG 26 "Schlageter"* commanded by Adolf Galland, which pilot added four Spitfires to his score of victories within a fortnight. Deliveries continued at a high rate, so that when on 22 June 1941 Germany marched against Russia, no less than 13 *Gruppen* had been re-equipped with the Bf 109F; these were three *Gruppen* of Major Johannes Trautloft's *JG 54* of *Luftflotte I* in Northern Russia; all four *Gruppen* of Werner Mölders' *JG 51*, and three *Gruppen* of Major Günther von Maltzahn's *JG 53 "Pik As"* of Kesselring's *Luftflotte II* in Central Russia; and three *Gruppen* of Major Günther Lützow's *JG 3 "Udet"* of Löhr's *Luftflotte IV* in Southern Russia. Within six weeks each of these *Jagdgeschwader* had attained the "1,000-victory" mark.

At the same time other units were taking Bf 109Fs on charge. On the Channel coast only two *Jagdgeschwader*

Bf 109F flown by the adjutant of III./JG 2 "Richthofen", Caen, France 1941. Note the upper surface camouflage has been carried over and slightly under the leading edge of the wing. (via M. C. Windrow)

remained. Three *Gruppen* of *JG 2* had received F-1s and F-2s, while *I* and *III Gruppen* of *JG 26 "Schlageter"* were mostly flying F-2s—later supplemented by a number of F-4s. The first Bf 109F to be shot down by the RAF is believed to have fallen to the guns of a No. 91 Squadron Spitfire VB on 11 May 1941, and 10 July—exactly a year after the first experimental flight—the first Bf 109F (an F-2) fell intact into British hands: Hauptmann Rolf Pingle, *Gruppenkommandeur* of *I/JG 26*, force-landed his aircraft near Dover, the fighter thereafter being repaired, and flown by British pilots.

By the time these *Jagdgeschwader* were required to provide air cover for the German warships *Scharnhorst*, *Gneisenau* and *Prinz Eugen,* escaping up the Channel on 11/12 February 1942, *JG 2* operated a total of 90 Bf 109F-4s, and *III/JG 26* included a strength of 30 Bf 109 F-4s. Later that year *10(Jabo)/JG 2*, a fighter-bomber *Staffel* equipped with Bf 109F-4/Bs carried out 32 raids in 60 days against targets in Southern England, led by Hauptmann Karl Plunser.

Notwithstanding these relatively limited activities in the West, the Bf 109F's main responsibilities lay in the East and in the Mediterranean theatre. The threat to Axis supply routes to North Africa posed by Malta in 1941 prompted the movement of *Luftflotte II* to the Mediterranean, and with it *JG 53 "Pik As"* and *II/JG 3 "Udet"*. The latter *Gruppe* and *I/JG 53* returned to Russia in May 1942, but *III/JG 53* moved to North Africa to join *JG 27*. These units at that time were almost exclusively equipped with tropicalised Bf 109F-2s and F-4s. The most celebrated German pilot of this period and theatre was undoubtedly Hans Joachim Marseille who as a Leutnant and ultimately *Staffelkapitän* of *3/JG 27*, was credited with 158 aerial victories before his death on 30 September 1942. Although at least sixty of these "victories" have since been positively discounted from minute examination of his claims in conjunction with actual losses recorded in Allied documents, there is no doubt that the prestige accorded to this young German pilot for propaganda purposes was not unwarranted for he was, in his Bf 109F-4/Trop, a superb fighter and a born pilot. He was, beyond dispute, by far the highest-scoring of all pilots in the Mediterranean theatre, and was a recipient of the Knight's Cross with Oakleaves, Swords and Diamonds.

On the Eastern Front the victory scores of Bf 109F pilots continued to mount rapidly. The eighth *Luftwaffe* pilot to reach a score of 100 victories was Oberleutnant Max-Hellmuth Ostermann, *Staffelkapitän* of *7/JG 54*, shooting down his 100th victim on 12 May 1942. The ninth such pilot was Hauptmann Heinz Bär, *Gruppenkommandeur* of *IV/JG 51 "Mölders"*, who reached this score on 19 May 1942; on the following day Major Gordon Gollob, *Kommodore* of *JG 77*, destroyed his 100th enemy aircraft.

One other operational expedient was pursued with the Bf 109F, that of improvised night interception. During the early summer nights of 1942 a few pilots of *JG 54* undertook night fighting sorties, the outstanding exponents being Hauptmann Joachim Wandel, *Staffelkapitän* of *5/JG 54*, who was credited with 16 night victories, and Oberleutnant Erwin Leykauf, who gained six such victims on a single night, that of 22/23 June 1942.

Germany also supplied a number of Bf 109Fs to her allies, Italy and Hungary. About forty F-2s and F-4s were supplied in 1942 to the Hungarian Air Force, whose pilots of the 1/1 Fighter Squadron had undergone training on the 109 with the *Luftwaffe* and were attached to the German air forces in the Stalingrad area. Shortly afterwards 5/1 and 5/2 Squadrons received a small number of F-4s, but these were quickly replaced by Bf 109Gs.

Early in 1943 the *3°* and *150° Gruppi Caccia Terrestre* of Italy's *Regia Aeronautica* received the Bf 109F, a variety of tropicalised F-4/Bs and F-4/R1s being supplied, and, based in Southern Italy and Sicily, these units were heavily engaged at the time of the Tunisian and Sicilian campaigns.

Development and experimental Bf 109Fs

While the Messerschmitt Bf 109G and H versions were developed in parallel, and stemmed from developed and modified Bf 109F airframes, a commentary on these basic versions should logically follow brief mention of some of the numerous experimental trials and expedients pursued with other Bf 109Fs. For example an early Bf 109F-1 (termed Bf 109V31 (*Werke Nr.* 5642, coded *SG+EK*) was used to test the wide-track undercarriage of the proposed Messerschmitt Me 209; the same aircraft later featured extended fairings from the wing trailing edges to house the cannon-breaches of the Me 209's proposed armament, and this aircraft went on to participate in the test programme for the proposed Me 309. It was joined in this programme by the original F-series *Vorsuchs* aircraft *VK+AB* which also tested engine cooling components in the Göppingen wind tunnel, while another aircraft (*Werke Nr.* 5603, coded *CE+EP*) tested the nosewheel undercarriages proposed for the Me 309 and Me 264 bomber. The Bf 109F V30 (*Werke Nr.* 5716, *ND+IE*) and V30a (*Werke Nr.* 5717, *ND+IF*) were test flown with cockpit pressurisation components for the Me 309. This project, finally seen to offer little substantial advance over the later Bf 109s, was however abandoned late in 1943.

Perhaps among the most striking variations of the Bf 109F was the experimental Bf 109F-4 (*Werke Nr.* 14003, *VJ+WC*) were fitted with a butterfly tail, i.e. "V" tail surfaces. Another F airframe was adapted to the radial BMW 801 engine for comparison with the standard DB 601E, and another was experimentally powered by a Junkers Jumo 213.

Finally there was the extraordinary *Beethoven-Gerät*—the mounting of a fighter (in this case a Bf 109F-4) atop an unmanned Junkers Ju 88A-4 bomber, modified to incorporate a fused 7,700-lb. warhead. All three engines would power the composite off the ground and to the target, where the Bf 109 pilot released his "flying bomb". A number of these weapons achieved operational status and were used with limited success immediately after D-Day in Northern Europe and elsewhere in 1944. At least one such weapon is known to have fallen in the vicinity of Maidstone, Kent, during the autumn of 1944.

The "Gustav"

Numerically by far the most important of all Bf 109 versions was the G-series, known familiarly as the "Gustav". This preponderance was principally because by the time the version was introduced the German aircraft industry

A Bf 109G-2Trop of III./JG 51 "Mölders" taxiing along the perimeter track on an airfield in Russia in 1943. Note the very heavy green dapple on the fuselage. (USAF via M. C. Windrow)

had been considerably expanded on account of material demands on three fronts: the huge conflagration of the Eastern Front, the erosion of Axis influence in the Mediterranean, and the ever-increasing Allied air offensive in the West.

Introduction of the Gustav was intended to be associated with use of the DB 605A engine which, by increasing the cylinder bore, compatible with existing bore centre-lines, and increasing the permissible engine speed, gave an output of 1,475 h.p. at sea level. However the new engine was not yet available for use in the 12 pre-production Bf 109G-Os, so that temporary recourse was made to the DB 601E. The initial production and service version, the G-1, was powered by the DB 605A-1 with GM-1 nitrous oxide injection to boost the engine's power above its rated altitude. Associated with the demand for more power at increased altitude was the use made of a pressure cabin together with local structual strengthening. The G-1/Trop, with tropical filters, changed to two 13-mm. MG 131 guns in place of the smaller and customary MG 17s in the nose decking, the new guns necessitating prominent breach fairing covers on either side of the upper nose decking—giving rise to the Gustav's other nickname—the *Beule* (="Bump").

After first appearance of the G-1 and G-1/Trop in all theatres during October and November 1942, variants began arriving in squadrons thick and fast. The G-2 was a medium-altitude reconnaissance fighter which omitted the pressure cabin and reverted to the MG 17 decking guns; it did however include provision for mounting two further *aft-firing* MG 17s in a detachable ventral gun pack—this remote-firing method of rearward defence being by no means unique on German aircraft. A sub-variant of this was the G-2/R1 fighter-bomber, which had provision for belly-shackles, to hold a 500-kilo bomb, and strongpoints for two underwing drop tanks. An interesting feature of this sub-variant was the occasional use of an auxiliary tail undercarriage leg to provide additional ground clearance, which would be jettisoned after take-off.

The pressurised G-3 reverted to the G-1s standard armament and differed only in the installation of FuG 16Z radio in place of the G-1s FuG 7A, while the G-4 was simply an unpressurised G-3.

A larger supercharger, MW-50 water-methanol injection into the cylinders together with use of 100-octane fuel increased the power of the DB 605D to 1,800 h.p., and this engine was introduced in the Bf 109G-5, which carried the water-methanol mixture in a jettisonable ventral tank. Armament was standardised as a hub-firing 20-mm. MG 151/20 cannon and two deck-mounted, synchronised 13-mm. MG 131 guns. The G-5/R2 introduced a wooden rudder and lengthened tail wheel oleo by which it was hoped to reduce the Gustav's tendency to swing on take-off, but the increased tail-weight necessitated the addition of a counterbalancing weight bolted in the nose under the oil tank bracket.

Most widely used of all Gustavs was the Bf 109G-6 which started to appear in the *Jagdgeschwader* in the spring of 1943. This was basically in effect a bomber-destroyer whose motivation was clearly the terrible portents of the day and night bomber offensive whose build-up was beginning to be felt during the winter of 1942-43. At crippling cost to the Gustav's previously fine performance, the armament of the G-6 (which was powered by either DB 605AM, AS, ASB, ASD or ASM engine) comprised two decking-mounted 13-mm. MG 131 guns, a hub-firing 30-mm. MK 108 cannon and two underwing 20-mm. MG 151/20 cannon. Top speed of this version was reduced to no more than 358 m.p.h. with DB 605 ASM engine. A further gun-fire increase was introduced with the G-6/U4 on which the underwing 20-mm. cannon were replaced by two further 30-mm. MK 108 cannon, while the G/6U4N night interceptor version (used on *Wilde Sau*—"Wild Boar"—operations by two *Jagdstaffeln* in the Cologne area) incorporated a Naxos-Z rotating direction-finding and homing antenna in a transparent blister aft of the cockpit.

Also introduced in 1943 was the G-6/R1 fighter-bomber capable of carrying either a 250-kilo SC 250 or 500-kilo SC 500 ventral bomb. The G-6/R2 featured a pair of under-wing 210-mm. WGr 21 *Dodel* rocket-launching tubes in place of the wing cannon and was used both for ground-attack and as a bomber-destroyer by *JG 1* and *JG 26 "Schlageter"*.

The G-7, which was intended to rationalise all previous effective modifications in one standard aircraft, did not achieve production status, the subsequent G-10 being preferred. The G-8 was a fast reconnaissance fighter with much reduced armament and either an RB 12.5/7 or RB 32/7 camera installed.

The excellent G-10 was the fastest of all Gustavs; powered by a DB 605D with GM-1 power boost, it possessed a top speed of 428 m.p.h. and an initial rate of climb of about 4,500 feet per minute, the good performance being achieved after deletion of the wing guns. In effect it matched all the best elements of performance of Allied fighters of 1943-44 and, in experienced hands, was capable of outfighting the P-51 Mustang (which, though faster, possessed a poor rate of climb by comparison) and the Spitfire IX (whose climb was comparable but which was significantly slower). Sub-variants included the Bf 109G-10/U4, with a belly-pack containing two 30-mm. MK 108 cannon with 80 rounds per gun (this was later replaced by a fixed long-range tank known as the *Irmer-Behälter*); and the G-10/R2 and R6 with wooden rudder, tail-oleo extension, FuG 25 "identification of friend or foe" radio, and a modified cabin canopy dubbed the "Galland hood".

Three other Gustav versions achieved production status. These were the G-12 (a tandem two-seat operational trainer derived by modification of a small number of G-1 airframes); the G-14 (the last Gustav to reach combat status and similar to the G-6 but with the "Galland hood"; sub-variants were the G-14/Trop and G-14/R2 with wooden rudder); and the G-16 armoured close-support fighter-bomber which, although it was in production at the end of the war, just failed to reach combat units.

A Bf 109F-4Trop of II./JG 53 "Pik As" in sand and green splotch camouflage with white spinner, fuselage band and upper and under wing tips taxiing out on a desert landing ground in Libya. (via Hans Redemann)

The last production series

Developed in parallel with the Gustav was the Bf 109H, also developed from the F-Series but far less widely used than either F or G. Basically the H-Series were intended for high-altitude work. Like the G-O, the H-O pre-production batch was ready too soon for the DB 605 and had to make do with DB 601E engines. The first H-1s were completed in 1943 and, powered by the DB 605A with GM-1 boost, were able to reach an altitude of 47,000 feet. Using a pressure cabin of course, the H-Series was chiefly identified by the greatly increased wing span—achieved by introducing additional wing sections which added 6 ft. 6 in. to the span—and strut-braced long-span tailplane. Armed with two nose-mounted MG 17s and a hub-firing 30-mm. MK 108 cannon, the H-1 was flown in France by a Service test group based at Guyancourt, and at one time a proposal was considered to add two 13-mm. MG 131 guns in the wings, but high-frequency oscillation of the long-span wings could not easily be cured and the proposal was dropped (as was the whole H-Series project) in favour of Kurt Tank's Focke-Wulf Ta 152H. There were other H-Series proposals—notably the Jumo 213E-powered H-2 and the Bf 109H-5 powered by a DB 605L engine—but neither entered production.

The next and last major variant after the H-Series was the K-Series (there being no I-Series, while the J-Series covered a stillborn proposal to licence-build the Gustav in Spain at the Barcelona works of Hispano).

By 1944 the Messerschmitt Bf 109 had long since passed the point at which its basic design was capable of matching contemporary Allied fighters by the customary and relatively simple expedients of increasing normal engine output and cleaning-up the profiles. While wholly-new generations of aircraft, such as the P-51 Mustang, Hawker Tempest and Supermarine (Griffon-powered) Spitfire XIV, had been developed with speeds much in excess of 400 m.p.h. inherent in their basic aerodynamics, Germany was forced to adopt design "fixes and crutches" in her relatively outmoded designs. It is of course true that some new-generation designs had appeared during the war—notably the Fw 190 and Me 210/410—but such had been the massive production tooling centred on the Bf 109 during 1943-44 that this fighter continued to be squeezed, stretched and boosted right up to the end of the Third Reich.

That is not to say that the Bf 109K—the last version to achieve production—was not an excellent fighter and a dangerous adversary, but in many areas of its performance envelope it was operating very close to the basic design limits. For example, considerable structure and equipment increases had brought about a 35% increase in wing loading, the landing speed had increased by 15 m.p.h.—and still the undercarriage was the relatively frail chassis of the early "Emil". Some measure of the reliance placed upon Willy Messerschmitt's venerable design can be gauged from progressive German production figures: 2,628 in 1941, 2,664 in 1942, 6,418 in 1943, and no fewer than 14,212 in 1944. Even in the few months of 1945, with factories bombed to rubble in the shrinking German perimeter, 2,969 were built.

Four variants in the K-Series reached production status, the K-2, the K-4, the K-6 and the K-14. After the customary pre-production batch of K-Os, the first K-2s

and K-4s reached squadrons early in 1944, both versions powered by the 1,500 h.p. rated DB 605 ASCM/DCM engine, MW 50-boosted to produce "spurts" at 2,000 h.p.; both were armed with two 15-mm. MG 151 and one 30-mm. MK 103 or 108 cannons, the sole difference between the variants being that the K-4 had a pressure cabin whereas the K-2 did not. The K-6 featured "bomber-destroyer" armament of two 13-mm. heavy machine guns in the nose-decking, a hub-firing 30-mm. MK 103 cannon and two underwing 30-mm. MK 103s.

The Bf 109K-14 was powered by a DB 605L with MW 50 boosting, bestowing a maximum speed of 450 m.p.h. Armament was decking-mounted 13-mm. MG 131s and a hub-firing 30-mm. MK 108. This was one of the versions that was in production in April and May 1945, but only two examples reached the Luftwaffe, being delivered to Stab II/JG 52 under Major Wilhelm Batz just before Germany's final surrender.

Mention must be made of a number of late 109 "odd-balls". The Bf 109L was a proposed development of the Gustav with an enlarged fuselage cross-section to accommodate a capsulated 1,750 h.p. Junkers Jumo 213E; with increased wing span, this version was expected to achieve 474 m.p.h. The Bf 109S was a proposed attempt to arrest the ever-increasing landing speeds of successive Bf 109s by recourse to blown flaps, one prototype (the Bf 109V 24, VK+AG) being in the process of conversion at the French Caudron-Renault factory when it fell into Allied hands late in 1944.

Other unbuilt projects included the proposed Bf 109TL jet-powered conversion and the Me 155A—a long-spanned DB 628-powered Gustav, intended to be capable of carrying a single 1,000-kilo (2,200 lb.) SC 1000 bomb. One project which reached the prototype stage but, as far as is known, was never flown was the Bf 109Z, devised to demonstrate the possibilities of the projected Messerschmitt Me 609. In essence it consisted of two Bf 109F fuselages (with port and starboard wings) and a new wing centre-section which joined the fuselages to form a single aeroplane. There is no doubt that the design philosophy of this project was no less imaginative than that of the North American F-82 Twin Mustang—which entered operational service half-a-dozen years later with another air force during another war.

The Gustav and others in service

The Gustav was first delivered to the newly-activated 11 Staffel of JG 2 "Richthofen" early in the summer of 1942, and it was in a Bf 109G-1/Trop of 3/JG 27 that Joachim Marseille met his death on 30 September that year after reporting fire in his aircraft while returning from a fighter strike in the Cairo area. By the end of the year the earlier F-Series had been almost entirely replaced by the Gustav, and in March 1943 III/JG 54 with 109Gs was withdrawn from the Eastern Front to combat the growing daylight raids by B-17s and B-24s of the USAAF. At the same time a new Jagdgeschwader, JG 11, was established out of a nucleus provided by I and III/JG 1. At the time of the German 1943 summer offensive on the Eastern Front (code named Zitadelle), which opened on 5 July, four ground-attack fighter Gruppen (II and III/JG 3, and I and III/JG 52) were equipped with Gustavs, and one of these, II/JG 3, claimed the destruction of 77 Russian aircraft on the first day—one pilot (Oblt. Joachim Kirschner) claiming no fewer than nine victories.

Also in 1943 the Gustav-equipped units of *Luftflotte 2* in the central Mediterranean theatre were under severe pressure, and included *Geschwader Stab*, I and III *Gruppen* of *JG 27*, II/*JG 51*, and *JG 53* and *JG 77*. Another Gustav unit was Obstlt. Günther Scholz's *Eismeerjagdgeschwader JG 5* based in Finland and Norway, whose four *Gruppen* all flew G-4s and G-6s until September 1943. In the Balkans the best-known Gustav units were Hauptman Hans Hahn's *I/JG 4*, based at Mitzil near Ploesti, and Oblt. Alfred Burk's *IV/JG 27* at Kalamaki in Greece. These provided the main fighter opposition to the 177 B-24 Liberators which attacked the Ploesti oilfields on 1 August 1943. By far the majority of the fifty-four B-24s shot down in this raid are thought to have fallen to the guns of *I/JG 4*.

Space does not permit mention of more than a small part of the defence provided by the Gustav against Allied attacks on Germany during 1943 and 1944. Suffice it to say that apart from the *Wilde Sau* night operations already mentioned, the *Jagdflieger* adopted numerous expedients against the Allied bombers (including bombing and ramming them in the air, both of which extreme tactics wrought heavy casualties among American airmen), and in 1944 their Gustavs were joined by the K-Series. At the time of the Allied landings in Normandy only two *Jagdgeschwader* were based in the immediate vicinity, but these were quickly reinforced by 23 *Jagdgruppen*, of which 13 were equipped with a total of about 400 Gustavs.

In Germany's last massive, desperate attack, the celebrated Operation "Herrmann" of 1 January 1945, by 750 fighters and fighter-bombers against Allied airfields in Northern Europe, the order of Battle included 12 *Gruppen* of Gustavs (I, III/*JG 3* with G-14s, I, III and IV/*JG 4* with G-6s, G-10s and G-14s, I, II/*JG 27* with G-6s and G-10s, I, II/*JG 53* with G-10s and G-14s, and I, II and III/*JG 77* with G-6s, G-10s and G-14s) and 5 *Gruppen* with K-Series (II/*JG 11* with K-4s, III and IV/*JG 27* with K-2s and K-4s, and III, IV/*JG 53* also with K-2s and K-4s).

Perhaps a measure of the desperation with which the *Jagdflieger* fought during those last moments of Hitler's *Reich* may be judged from the actions of *Rammkommando Elbe*—a Gustav-equipped unit of volunteers led by Oberst Hajo Herrmann, who attacked enemy bomber formations by ramming, it being intended that the Gustav pilot would bale out at the last moment. On 7 April 1945, 120 such pilots took off against an American bomber formation—and only 15 returned.

Foreign service

Foreign service and manufacture of the late-series Bf 109 was fairly widespread. 145 Gustavs were delivered to **Bulgaria** in 1943-1944 and served with the Sixth Fighter Regiment of the Bulgarian Air Force in defence of Sofia in April 1944. About a dozen G-10s were flown by **Croat** pilots in the 15 (Croat) *Staffel* of *JG 52*, led by Obstlt. Fanjo Dzal, which fought in *Zitadelle*.

Slovakia received fifteen Gustavs in 1944 and licence-production was planned of the G-14 at the Prague-Cakovice Avia factory, but only after the war, with the re-establishment of the **Czechoslovak** nation, did the first complete G-14 (designated the Avia C-10) emerge. The C-110 two-seat trainer accompanied the C-10 into service with the Czech Air Force, but shortage of DB 605 engines soon ended the career of this version. Use of the alternative Jumo 211F engine necessitated much redesign and, with a heavy, paddle-bladed propeller, the new "109" entered service as the S-199 fighter and CS-199 trainer. In March 1948 several C-210s were sold by Czechoslovakia to **Israel** and these were fought against the Egyptian Air Force. S-199s remained in service with the Czech National Security Guard until 1957.

Finland received 30 Bf 109G-2s, 132 G-6s and a few G-14s (the latter abandoned by the retreating Germans in 1944), and the first unit thus equipped was HLeLv 34 based at Utti in 1943. They were flown by such outstanding Finnish aces as Juutulainen (94 victories) and Hasse Wind (78 victories). These Gustavs remained in service until replaced by D.H. Vampires in 1952.

The Royal **Hungarian** Air Force received 59 German-made Gustavs in addition to about 700 aircraft built at factories at Gyor and Budapest. The first units to receive these fighters were the 5/1. and 5/2. Squadrons of the 5/I. Fighter Group, fighting on the Russian Front. Later on the 5/1. Squadron was withdrawn and the 5/2. Squadron expanded to form the 102nd. Independent Fighter Squadron. In 1944 the 101st. Fighter Group, known as the "Puma" Group under Obstlt. Alador Heppes, was established to defend Hungary itself against the advancing Russian forces.

Rumania received seventy Gustavs (principally G-8s) from Germany in addition to sixteen built at the IAR factory at Brasnov before it was destroyed by bombing, but the armed forces of Rumania had been so weakened by 1944 that these fighters contributed little in the defence of the country.

Spain has used the Bf 109 and its derivatives longer than any other country, since the debut of the Bf 109B during the Civil War in 1937. During the Second World War the country received a total of 95 airframes and these entered service with Spanish engines and under Spanish designations; they included 45 Bf 109Bs (designated C-4s), 15 Bf 109Es (C-5s), 10 Bf 109Fs (C-10s) and 25 Bf 109Gs (C-12s). Subsequently Bf 109G airframes were further adapted to take the Hispano Suiza 12-Z-89 engine, and later still the 12-Z-17, the Spanish-built versions being designated HA 1109-K1L, 1110-K1L and 1112-K1L. When supplies of the Hispano engine ceased, subsequent Spanish production of the "109" continued, then being adapted to take the Rolls-Royce Merlin.

Switzerland's procurement of twelve G-6s from Germany is a macabre story, for these fighters were supplied in return for the destruction of a radar-equipped Messerschmitt Bf 110G-4/R7 night fighter which made a force-landing at Dubendorf on 28 April 1944. The G-6s (plus a further two which were sequestrated after straying into Swiss air space) were delivered to *Fliegerkompagnie 7*, but owing to Germany's own production problems they were seldom in an operational state due to a chronic lack of spares.

Left: Nose detail of a Bf 109G-6 of JG 77 in South Russia. (Hans Obert)

Below: A pair of Bf 109G-6/R2s with WGr.21 rocket launching tubes under each wing mainly used for bomber-interception operations. (F. Selinger)

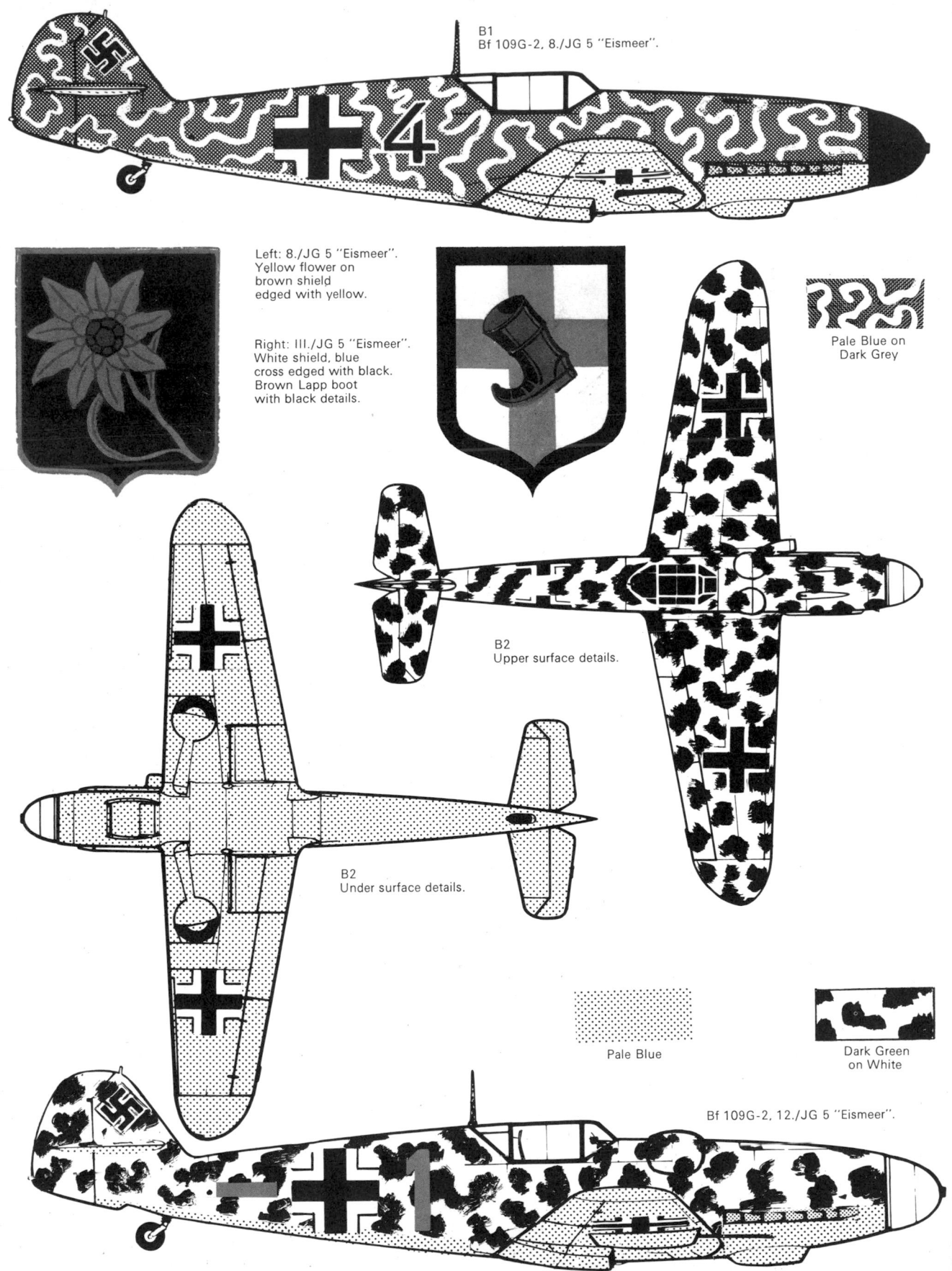

B1
Bf 109G-2, 8./JG 5 "Eismeer".

Left: 8./JG 5 "Eismeer".
Yellow flower on
brown shield
edged with yellow.

Right: III./JG 5 "Eismeer".
White shield, blue
cross edged with black.
Brown Lapp boot
with black details.

Pale Blue on
Dark Grey

B2
Upper surface details.

B2
Under surface details.

Pale Blue

Dark Green
on White

Bf 109G-2, 12./JG 5 "Eismeer".

Above: 6./JG 53 "Pik As" scrambling on a Sicilian airfield in early 1943. The upper surfaces of these Bf 109G-2s are in the standard splinter camouflage but the fuselage sides have been sprayed with sand, usually during the closing weeks of the Tunisian campaign and subsequent operations from Sicily replacement aircraft were left in the camouflage they arrived in receiving the white theatre markings only, and not always them. (USAF via M. C. Windrow)

Above: A damaged Bf 109G of 6./JG 53 in a sand-bagged revetment on a Sicilian airfield. As the above this aircraft has also been sprayed sand along the fuselage sides with green dapple breaking up the hard demarcation line along the aft fuselage. Wing upper surfaces sometimes received a rough sand dapple on the green splinter camouflage which appears to have been done on this aircraft. Note both the upper and under wing tips have been painted white, this theatre marking was usually only applied to the under surfaces. White spinner, fuselage band, 11 and bar. (IWM via C. F. Shores)

Below: A Bf 109F-4 of 6./JG 53 "Pik As" in rather scruffy white winter scheme. See D2 for colour details. (R. Ward)

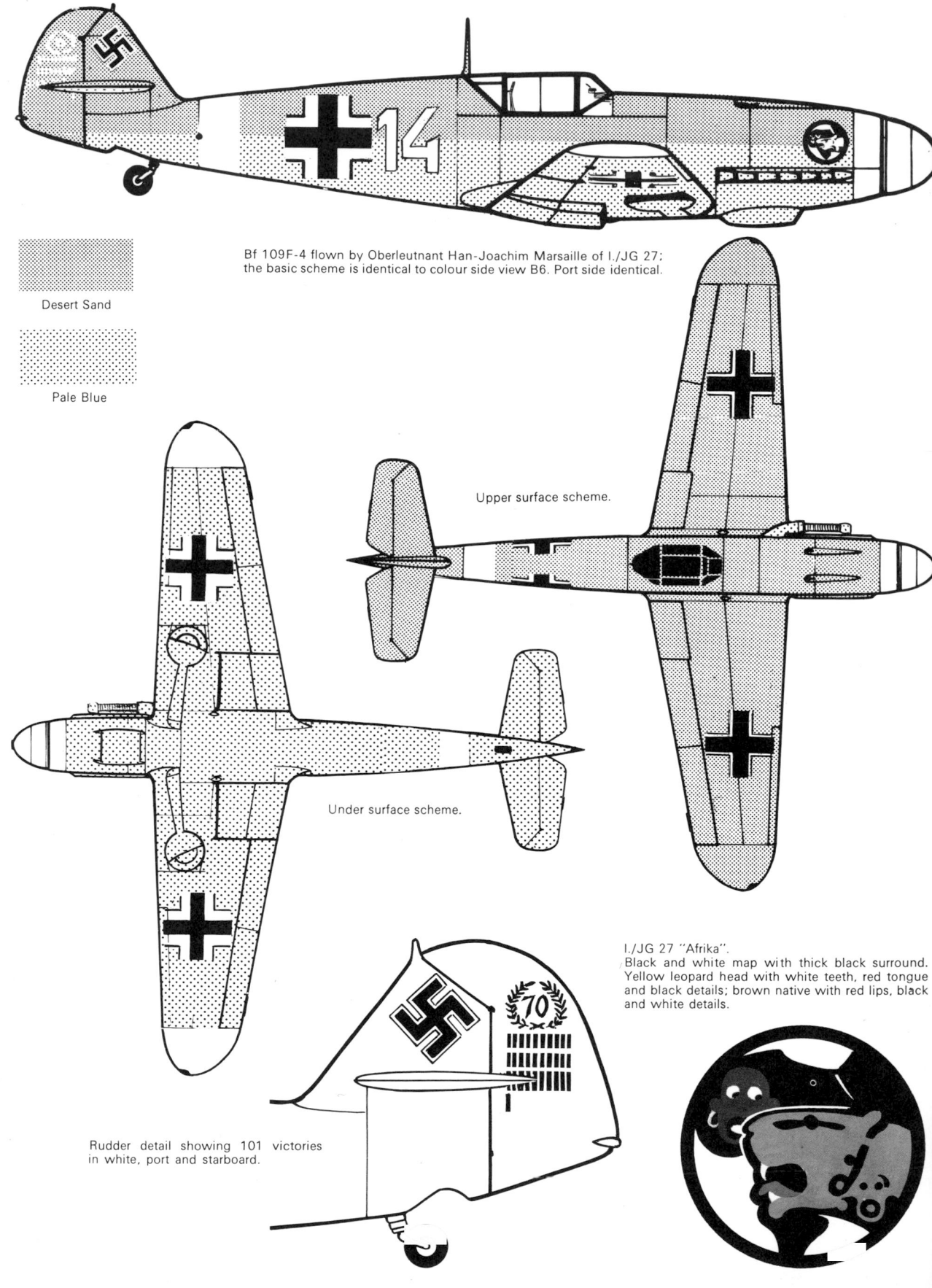

Bf 109F-4 flown by Oberleutnant Han-Joachim Marsaille of I./JG 27; the basic scheme is identical to colour side view B6. Port side identical.

Desert Sand

Pale Blue

Upper surface scheme.

Under surface scheme.

I./JG 27 "Afrika".
Black and white map with thick black surround. Yellow leopard head with white teeth, red tongue and black details; brown native with red lips, black and white details.

Rudder detail showing 101 victories in white, port and starboard.

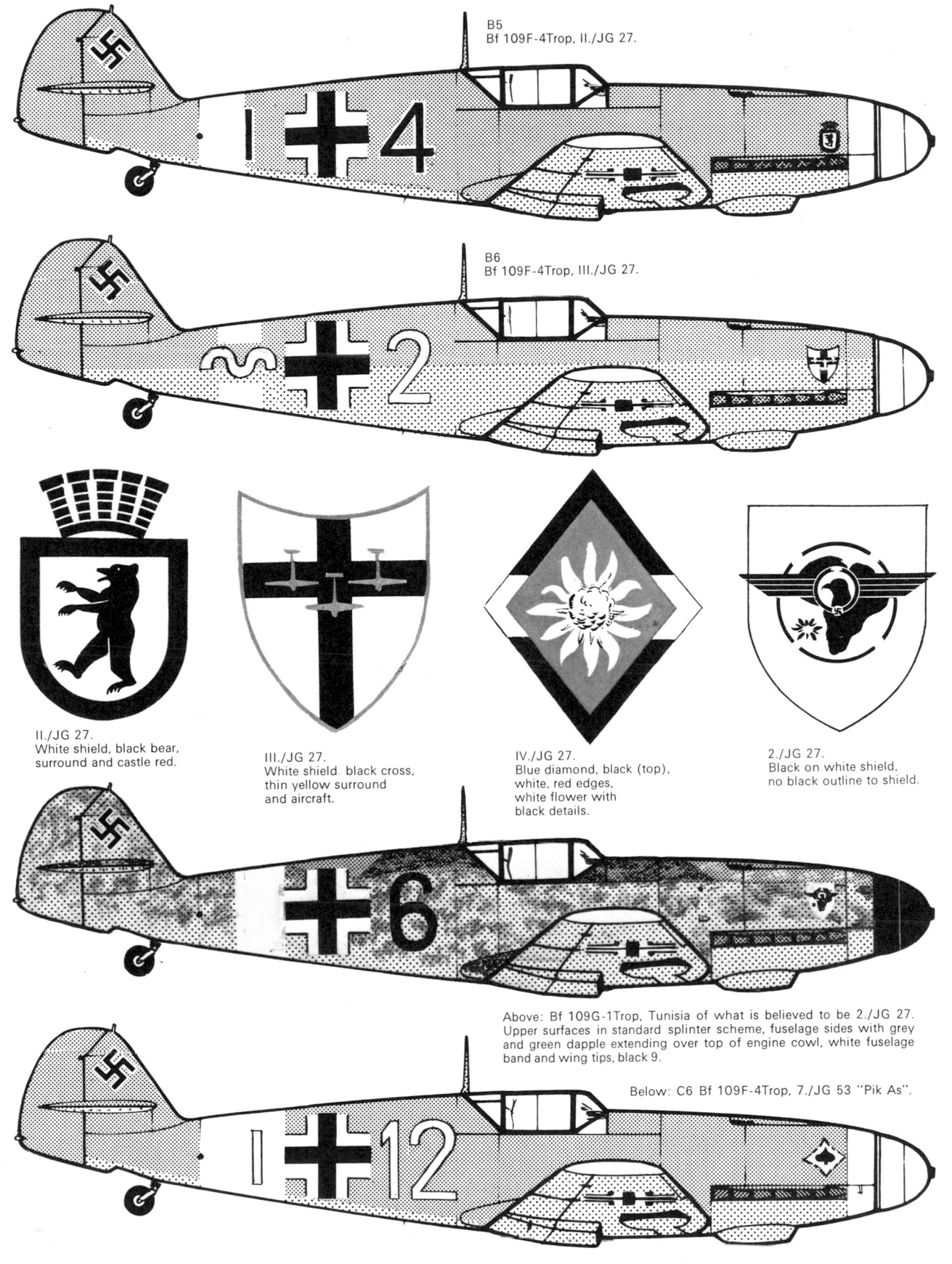

B5
Bf 109F-4Trop, II./JG 27.

B6
Bf 109F-4Trop, III./JG 27.

II./JG 27.
White shield, black bear,
surround and castle red.

III./JG 27.
White shield, black cross,
thin yellow surround
and aircraft.

IV./JG 27.
Blue diamond, black (top),
white, red edges,
white flower with
black details.

2./JG 27.
Black on white shield,
no black outline to shield.

Above: Bf 109G-1Trop, Tunisia of what is believed to be 2./JG 27.
Upper surfaces in standard splinter scheme, fuselage sides with grey
and green dapple extending over top of engine cowl, white fuselage
band and wing tips, black 9.

Below: C6 Bf 109F-4Trop, 7./JG 53 "Pik As".

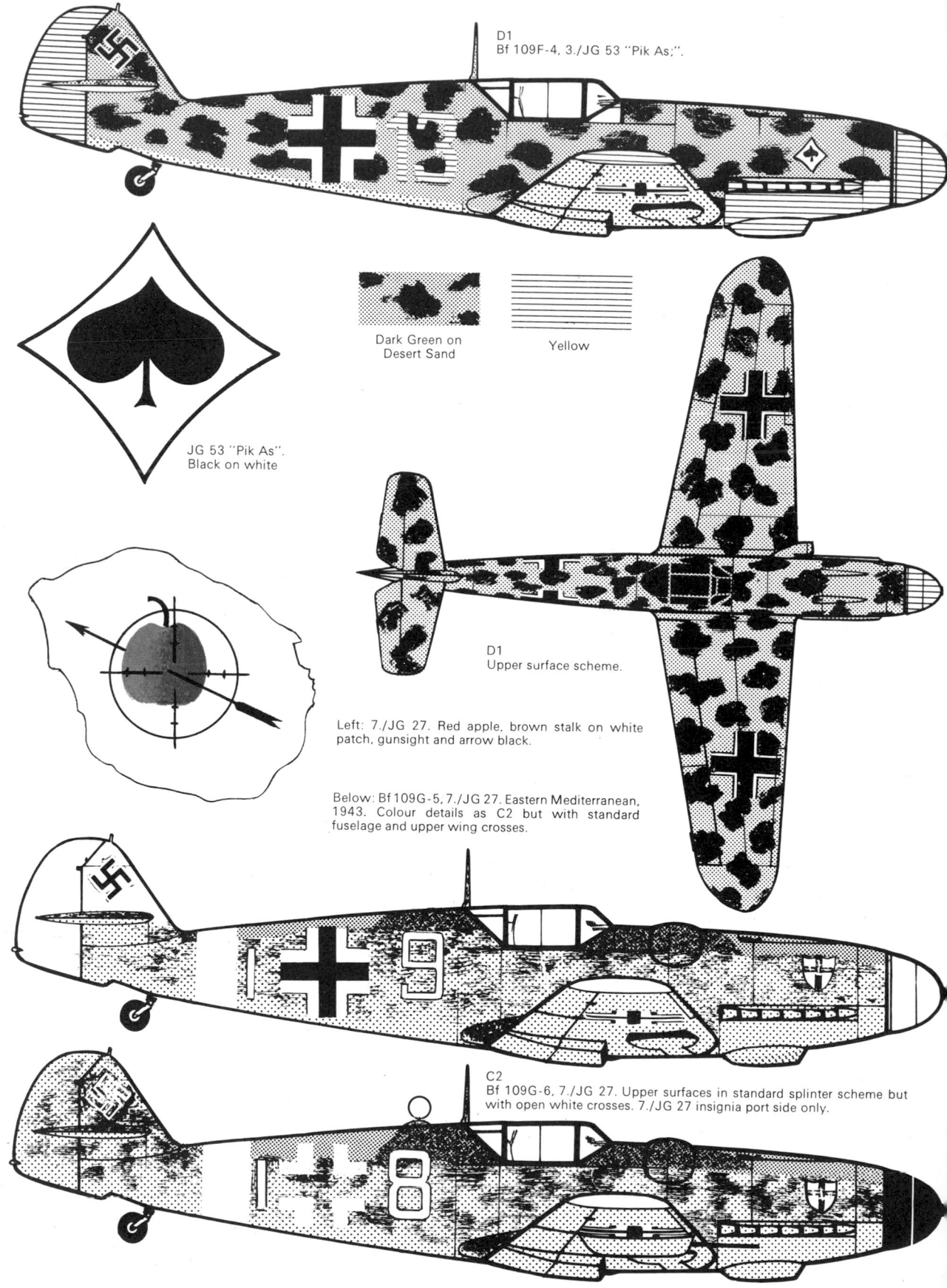

D1
Bf 109F-4, 3./JG 53 "Pik As;".

Dark Green on
Desert Sand

Yellow

JG 53 "Pik As".
Black on white

D1
Upper surface scheme.

Left: 7./JG 27. Red apple, brown stalk on white
patch, gunsight and arrow black.

Below: Bf 109G-5, 7./JG 27. Eastern Mediterranean,
1943. Colour details as C2 but with standard
fuselage and upper wing crosses.

C2
Bf 109G-6, 7./JG 27. Upper surfaces in standard splinter scheme but
with open white crosses. 7./JG 27 insignia port side only.

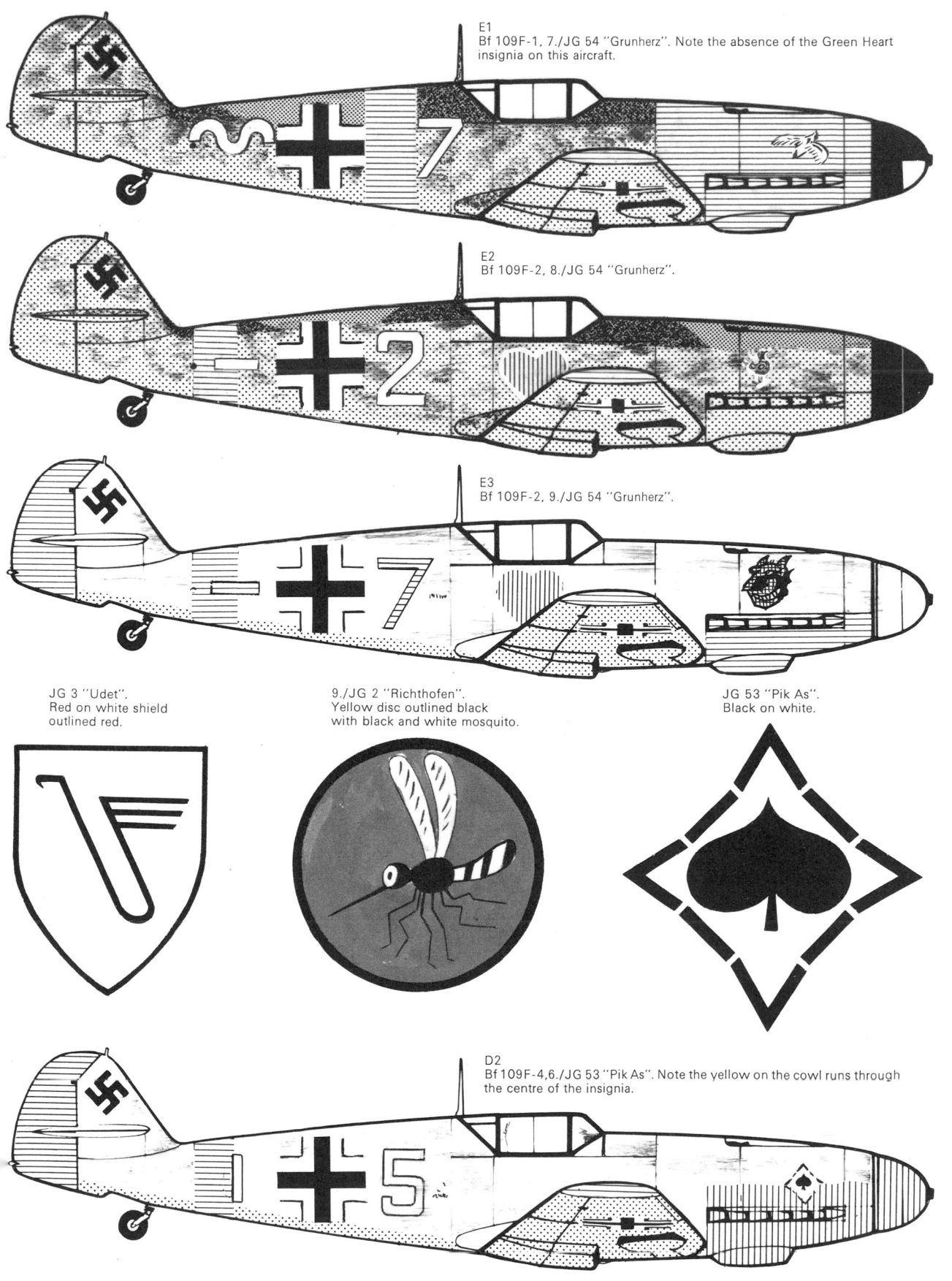

E1
Bf 109F-1, 7./JG 54 "Grunherz". Note the absence of the Green Heart insignia on this aircraft.

E2
Bf 109F-2, 8./JG 54 "Grunherz".

E3
Bf 109F-2, 9./JG 54 "Grunherz".

JG 3 "Udet".
Red on white shield
outlined red.

9./JG 2 "Richthofen".
Yellow disc outlined black
with black and white mosquito.

JG 53 "Pik As".
Black on white.

D2
Bf 109F-4, 6./JG 53 "Pik As". Note the yellow on the cowl runs through the centre of the insignia.

A Bf 109F-4 of I./JG 54 "Grunherz" dispersed amongst the trees on a Finnish airfield. Note the heavy dapple along the fuselage side, white 11 with thin black outline. Few photographs of Bf 109Fs in the marking of I./JG 54 have appeared in print. (B. Hielm)

Above: Bf 109G-2s of III./JG 54 "Grunherz" on an airfield in Russia, white 1 and 6. Fuselage sides in typical JG 54 green and black-green scheme. (T. M. Thoronsen)

Right: Major Hannes Trautloft of JG 54 standing alongside his Bf 109G-2 after an op over the Russian front lines. Typical JG 54 fuselage scheme. (Hans Obert)

Bf 109F-4s being serviced on a Russian airfield during the 1942–43 winter. (R. Ward)

A Bf 109G-2 of III./JG 53 "Pik As". Note the Geschwader insignia, with solid outline on the cowl and black and white spinner. Standard camouflage scheme. (Franz Selinger via M. C. Windrow)

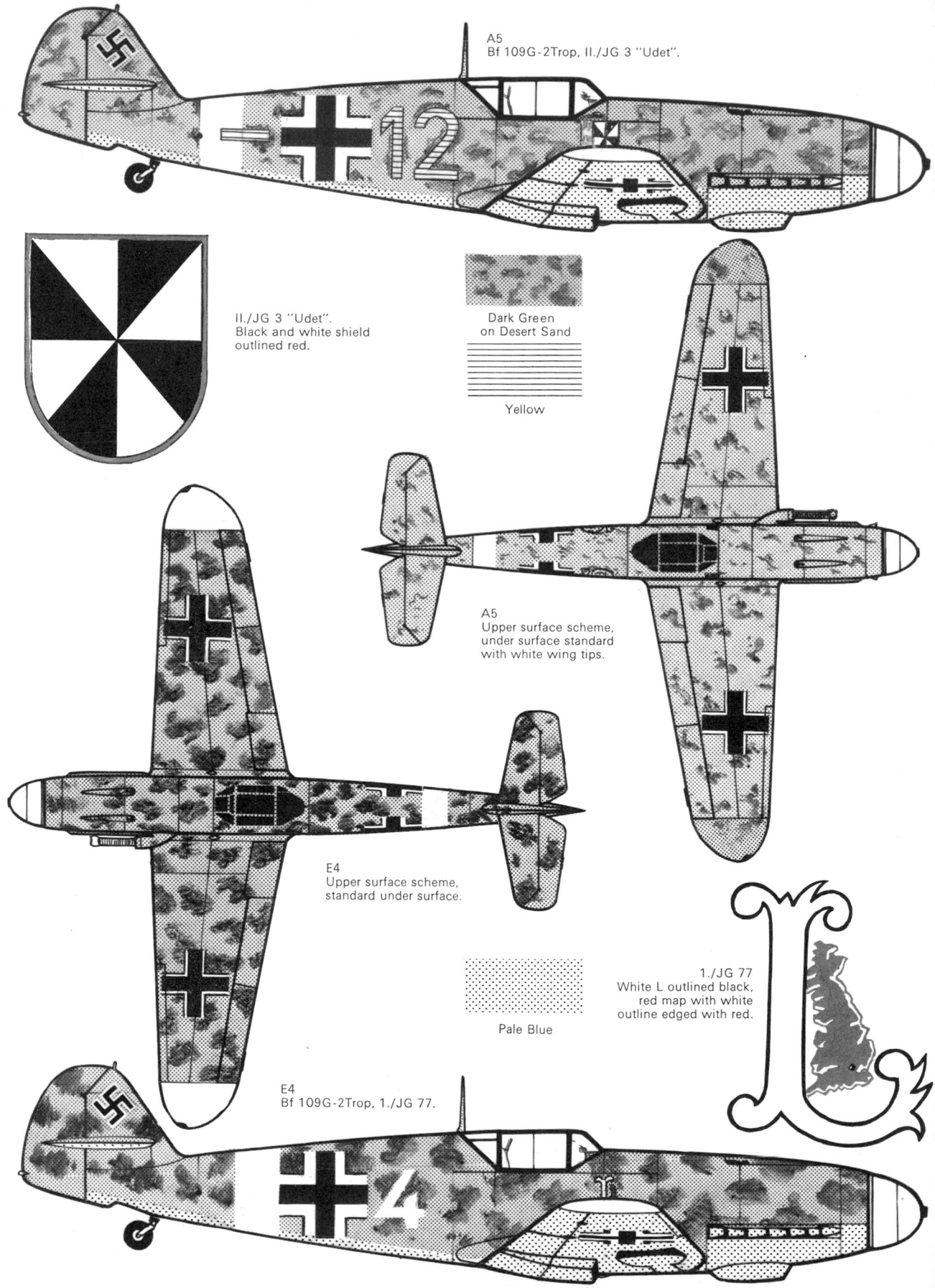

A5
Bf 109G-2Trop, II./JG 3 "Udet".

II./JG 3 "Udet".
Black and white shield
outlined red.

Dark Green
on Desert Sand

Yellow

A5
Upper surface scheme,
under surface standard
with white wing tips.

E4
Upper surface scheme,
standard under surface.

1./JG 77
White L outlined black,
red map with white
outline edged with red.

Pale Blue

E4
Bf 109G-2Trop, 1./JG 77.

Above, left: Nose detail of Bf 109G-1Trop of 2./JG 27, note the grey dapple is carried over the top of the cowl. (IWM)

Above, right: The insignia of II./JG 27 on the nose of a desert Bf 109F-4Trop. (IWM)

Above: A Bf 109F of I./JG 27 in standard sand and pale blue scheme, note absence of white wing tips. (IWM)

Below: A Bf 109G probably of 6./JG 53 "Pik As" being serviced on an airfield in Sicily. (USAF via M. C. Windrow)

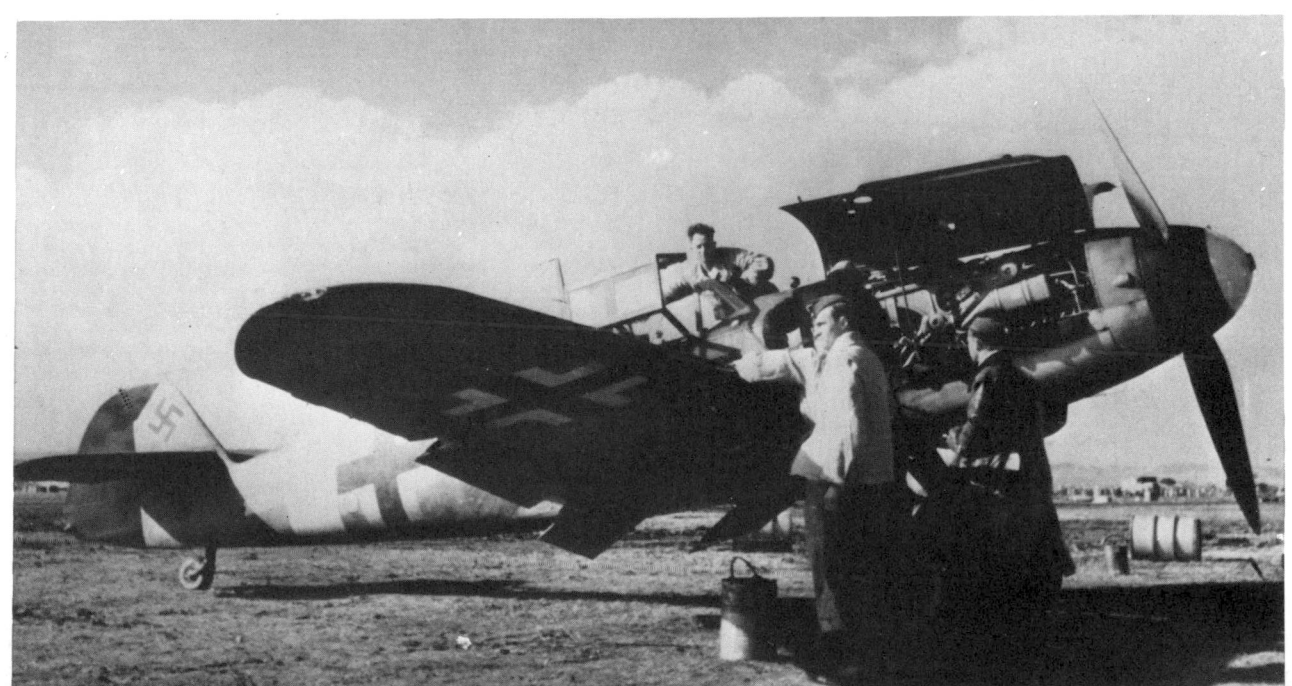

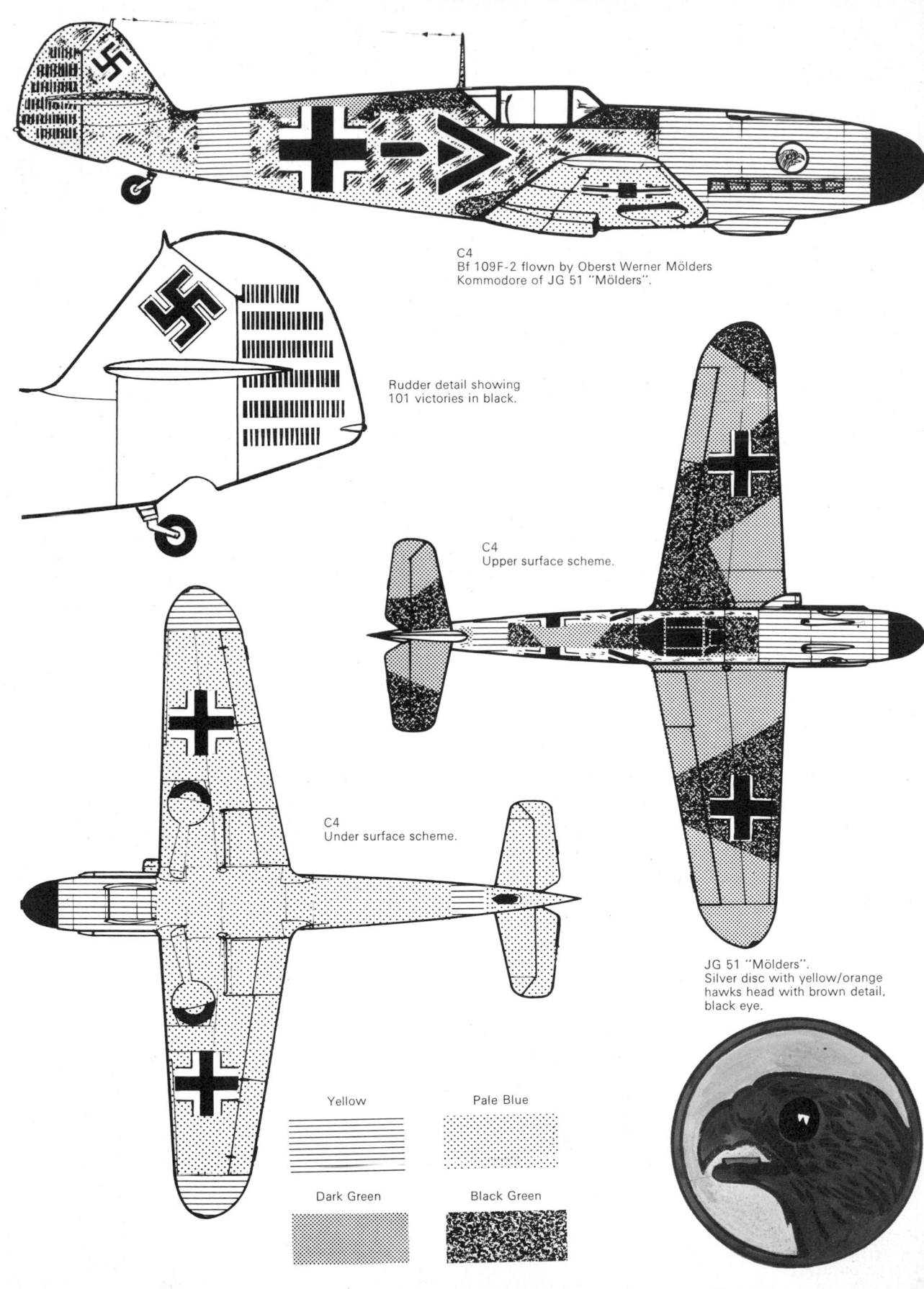

C4
Bf 109F-2 flown by Oberst Werner Mölders
Kommodore of JG 51 "Mölders".

Rudder detail showing
101 victories in black.

C4
Upper surface scheme.

C4
Under surface scheme.

JG 51 "Mölders".
Silver disc with yellow/orange
hawks head with brown detail,
black eye.

Yellow

Pale Blue

Dark Green

Black Green

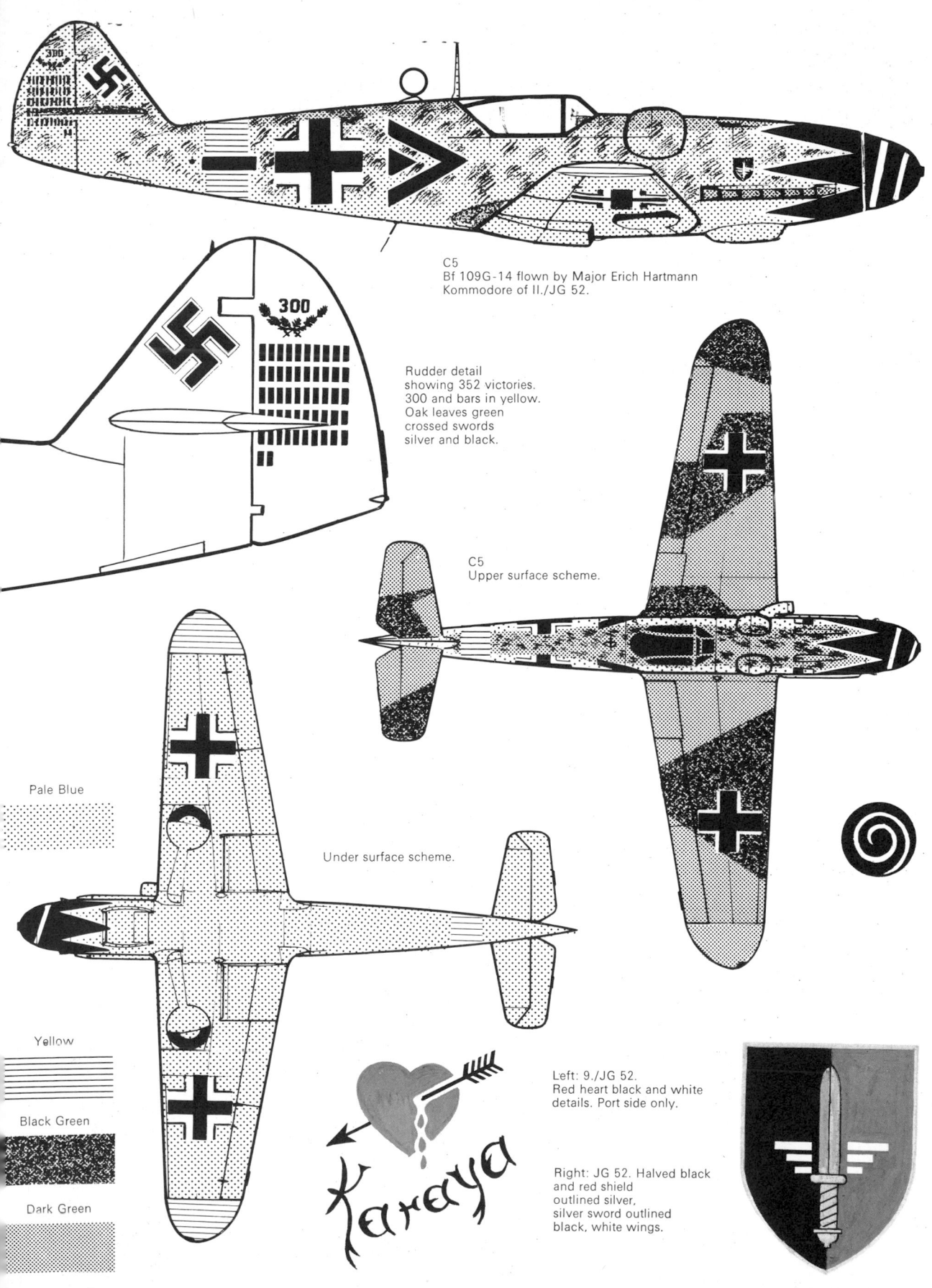

C5
Bf 109G-14 flown by Major Erich Hartmann
Kommodore of II./JG 52.

Rudder detail
showing 352 victories.
300 and bars in yellow.
Oak leaves green
crossed swords
silver and black.

C5
Upper surface scheme.

Under surface scheme.

Pale Blue

Yellow

Black Green

Dark Green

Left: 9./JG 52.
Red heart black and white
details. Port side only.

Right: JG 52. Halved black
and red shield
outlined silver,
silver sword outlined
black, white wings.

Karaya

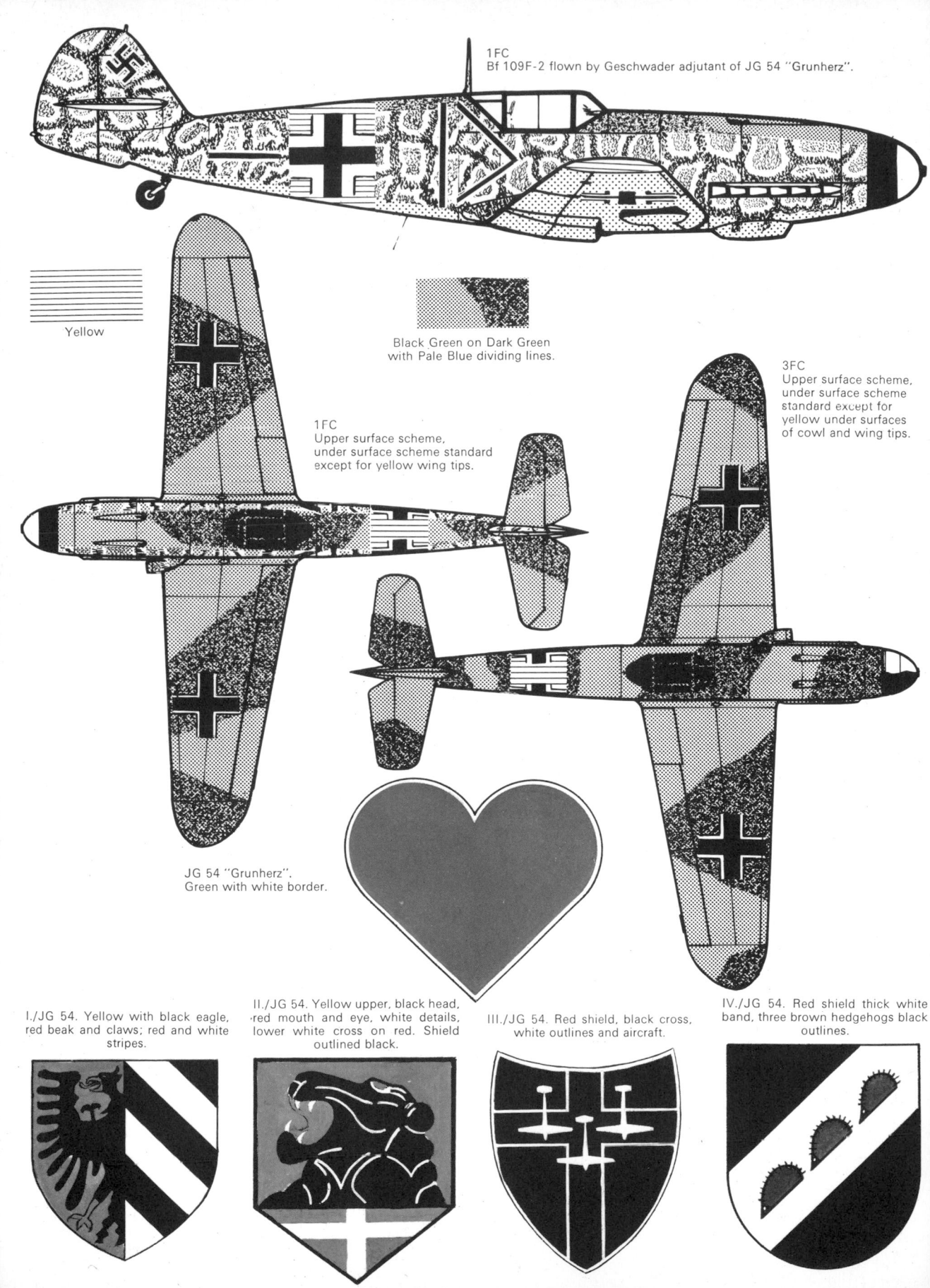

1FC
Bf 109F-2 flown by Geschwader adjutant of JG 54 "Grunherz".

Yellow

Black Green on Dark Green with Pale Blue dividing lines.

3FC
Upper surface scheme, under surface scheme standard except for yellow under surfaces of cowl and wing tips.

1FC
Upper surface scheme, under surface scheme standard except for yellow wing tips.

JG 54 "Grunherz". Green with white border.

I./JG 54. Yellow with black eagle, red beak and claws; red and white stripes.

II./JG 54. Yellow upper, black head, red mouth and eye, white details, lower white cross on red. Shield outlined black.

III./JG 54. Red shield, black cross, white outlines and aircraft.

IV./JG 54. Red shield thick white band, three brown hedgehogs black outlines.

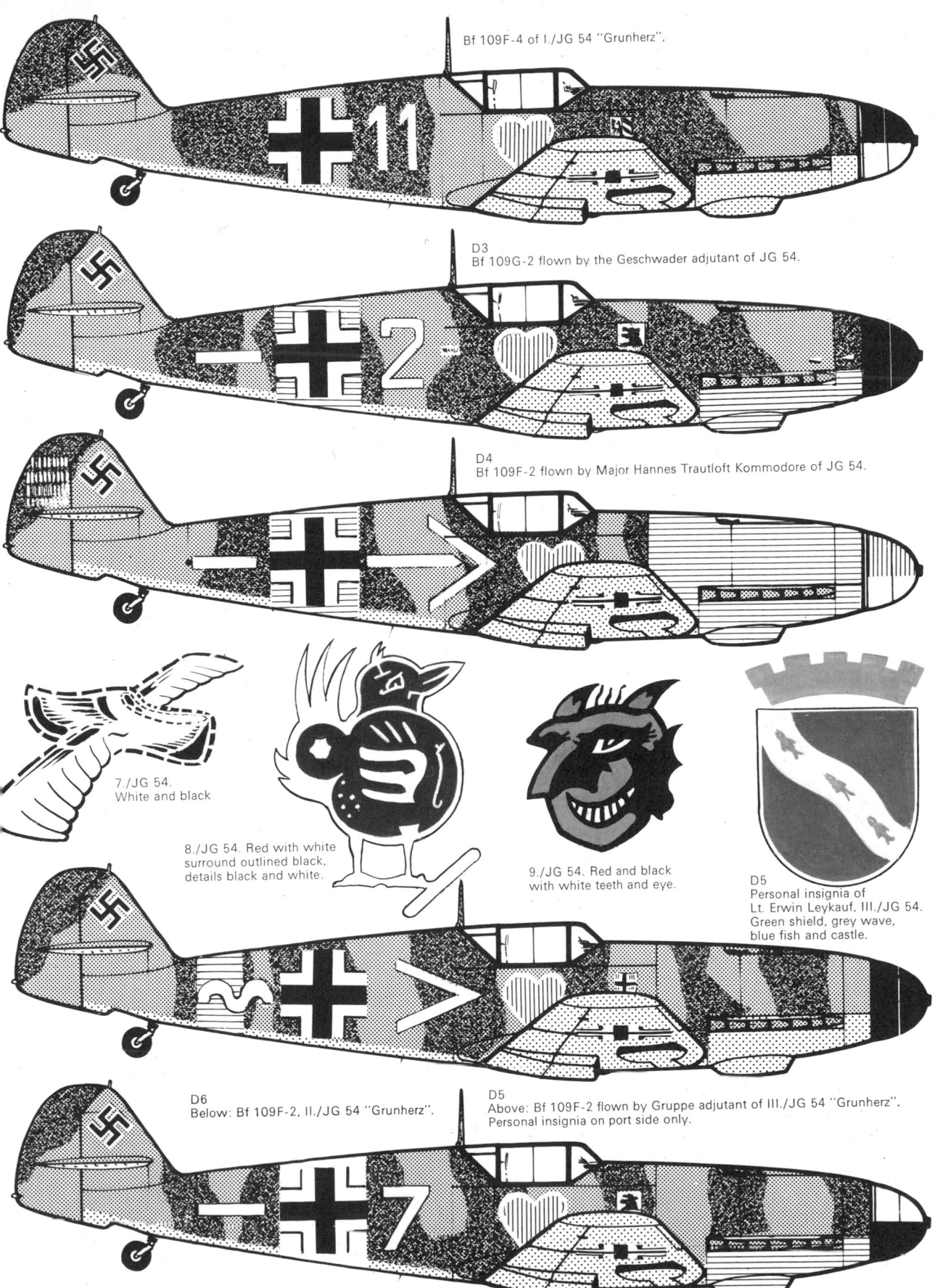

Bf 109F-4 of I./JG 54 "Grunherz".

D3
Bf 109G-2 flown by the Geschwader adjutant of JG 54.

D4
Bf 109F-2 flown by Major Hannes Trautloft Kommodore of JG 54.

7./JG 54.
White and black

8./JG 54. Red with white
surround outlined black,
details black and white.

9./JG 54. Red and black
with white teeth and eye.

D5
Personal insignia of
Lt. Erwin Leykauf, III./JG 54.
Green shield, grey wave,
blue fish and castle.

D6
Below: Bf 109F-2, II./JG 54 "Grunherz".

D5
Above: Bf 109F-2 flown by Gruppe adjutant of III./JG 54 "Grunherz".
Personal insignia on port side only.

Above: Two of the first batch of Bf 109G-2s for the Finnish Air Force arriving at Utti in March 1943. The nearest aircraft GD+UY later became MT-214. (via Eino Ritaranta)

Above: MT-201, first of the G-2s in full Finnish markings. (via Eino Ritaranta)

Below: Bf 109G-6, MT-453 of HLeLv 34 dispersed on Taipalsaari airfield during July 1944. Note white 11 just ahead of cockpit. (via Borje Hielm)

Top: A Bf 109G-2 after a forced landing during the winter of 1943. (via Borje Hielm)

Above: MT-201 a Bf 109G-2 taxiing out for take-off at Utti in March 1943 shortly after delivery. MT-201 was the personal aircraft of Major E. Luukkanen. (via Eino Ritaranta)

Left: MT-210 on the tarmac at Malmi airport, Helsinki. (via Eino Ritaranta)

Below: Bf 109G-2, MT-222 of HLeLv 34 photographed during the summer of 1943. In the background is the Douglas DC-2, DO-1 "Hanssin-Jukka". (via Borje Hielm)

Above: Bf 109G-6 photographed during the spring of 1944. (via Borje Hielm)

Above: Bf 109G-6, MT-435 of 3/HLeLv 34, note the white 1 ahead of cockpit, distant aircraft has a white 8 in the same position. (via Borje Hielm)

Left: Bf 109G-2, MT-216 on the dispersal area at Utti, note the fin and rudder have been heavily overpainted. (via Eino Ritaranta)

Below: Lt. Nils Katajainen standing alongside his Bf 109G-6, MT-506. White 8 ahead of cockpit, Galland hood. (via Borje Hielm)

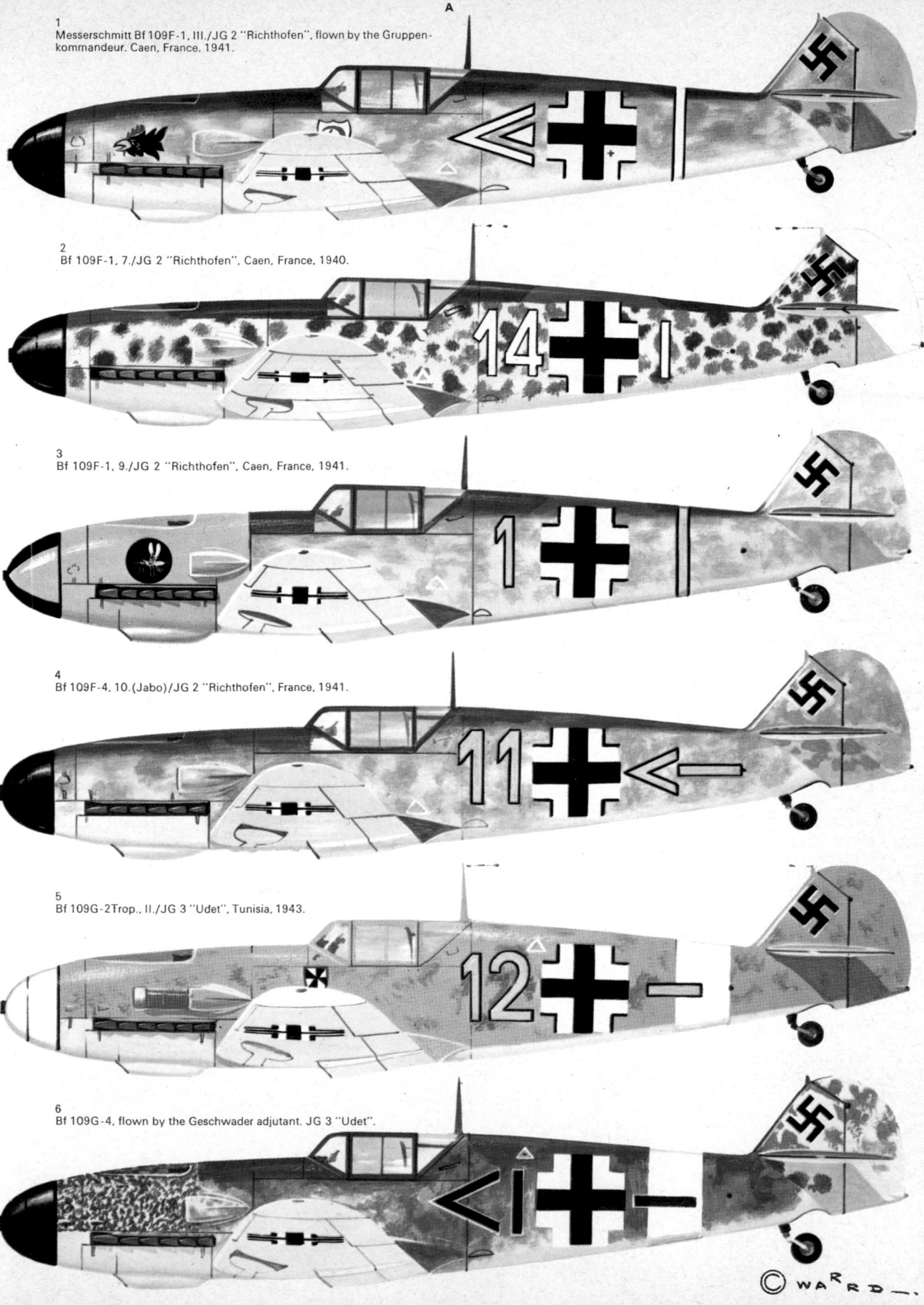

1
Messerschmitt Bf 109F-1, III./JG 2 "Richthofen", flown by the Gruppen-kommandeur. Caen, France, 1941.

2
Bf 109F-1, 7./JG 2 "Richthofen", Caen, France, 1940.

3
Bf 109F-1, 9./JG 2 "Richthofen", Caen, France, 1941.

4
Bf 109F-4, 10.(Jabo)/JG 2 "Richthofen", France, 1941.

5
Bf 109G-2Trop., II./JG 3 "Udet", Tunisia, 1943.

6
Bf 109G-4, flown by the Geschwader adjutant. JG 3 "Udet".

© WARRD

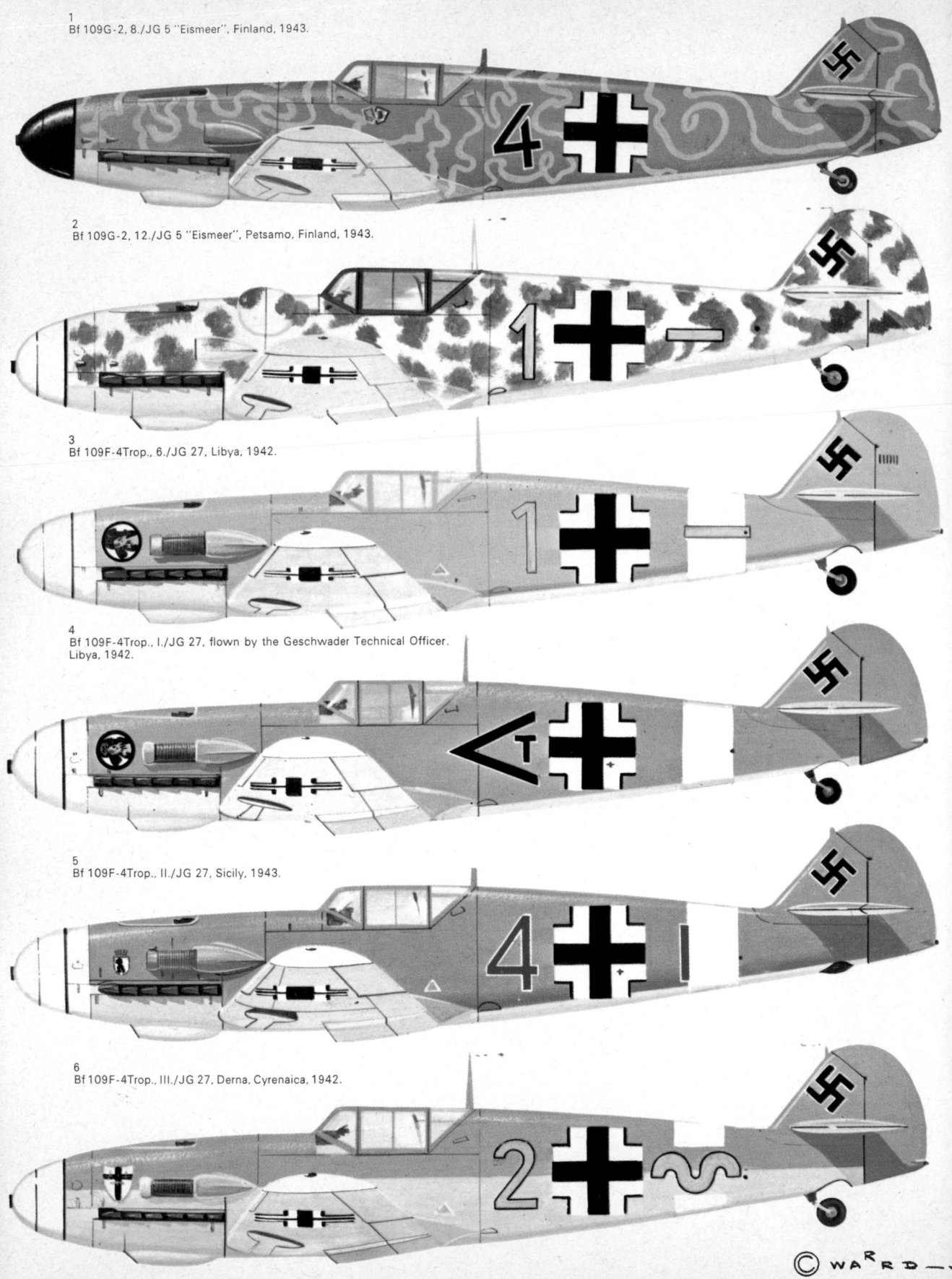

B

1
Bf 109G-2, 8./JG 5 "Eismeer", Finland, 1943.

2
Bf 109G-2, 12./JG 5 "Eismeer", Petsamo, Finland, 1943.

3
Bf 109F-4Trop., 6./JG 27, Libya, 1942.

4
Bf 109F-4Trop., I./JG 27, flown by the Geschwader Technical Officer. Libya, 1942.

5
Bf 109F-4Trop., II./JG 27, Sicily, 1943.

6
Bf 109F-4Trop., III./JG 27, Derna, Cyrenaica, 1942.

© WARRD

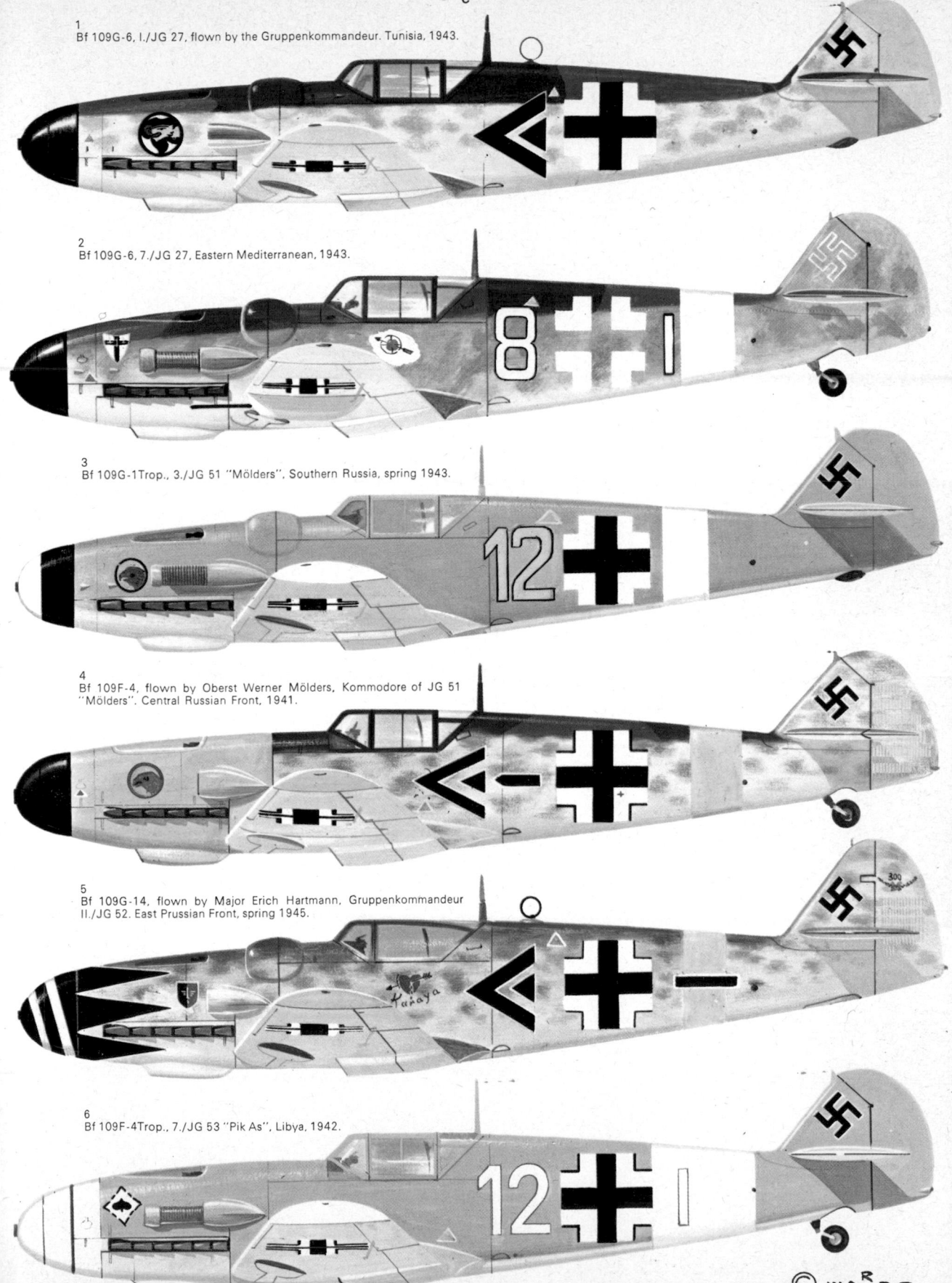

c

1
Bf 109G-6, I./JG 27, flown by the Gruppenkommandeur. Tunisia, 1943.

2
Bf 109G-6, 7./JG 27, Eastern Mediterranean, 1943.

3
Bf 109G-1Trop., 3./JG 51 "Mölders", Southern Russia, spring 1943.

4
Bf 109F-4, flown by Oberst Werner Mölders, Kommodore of JG 51 "Mölders". Central Russian Front, 1941.

5
Bf 109G-14, flown by Major Erich Hartmann, Gruppenkommandeur II./JG 52. East Prussian Front, spring 1945.

6
Bf 109F-4Trop., 7./JG 53 "Pik As", Libya, 1942.

© WARD

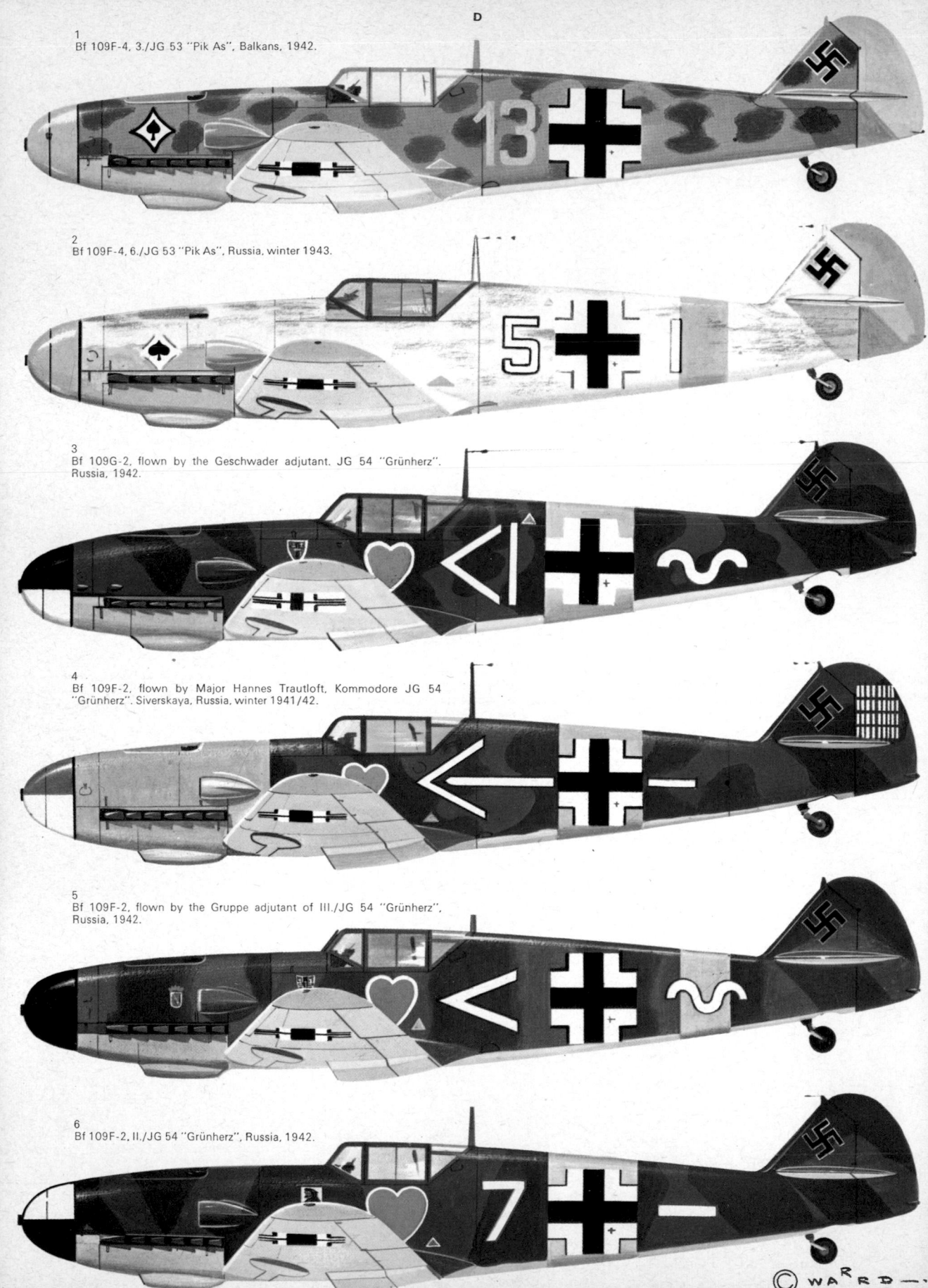

D

1
Bf 109F-4, 3./JG 53 "Pik As", Balkans, 1942.

2
Bf 109F-4, 6./JG 53 "Pik As", Russia, winter 1943.

3
Bf 109G-2, flown by the Geschwader adjutant. JG 54 "Grünherz". Russia, 1942.

4
Bf 109F-2, flown by Major Hannes Trautloft, Kommodore JG 54 "Grünherz". Siverskaya, Russia, winter 1941/42.

5
Bf 109F-2, flown by the Gruppe adjutant of III./JG 54 "Grünherz", Russia, 1942.

6
Bf 109F-2, II./JG 54 "Grünherz", Russia, 1942.

© WARD

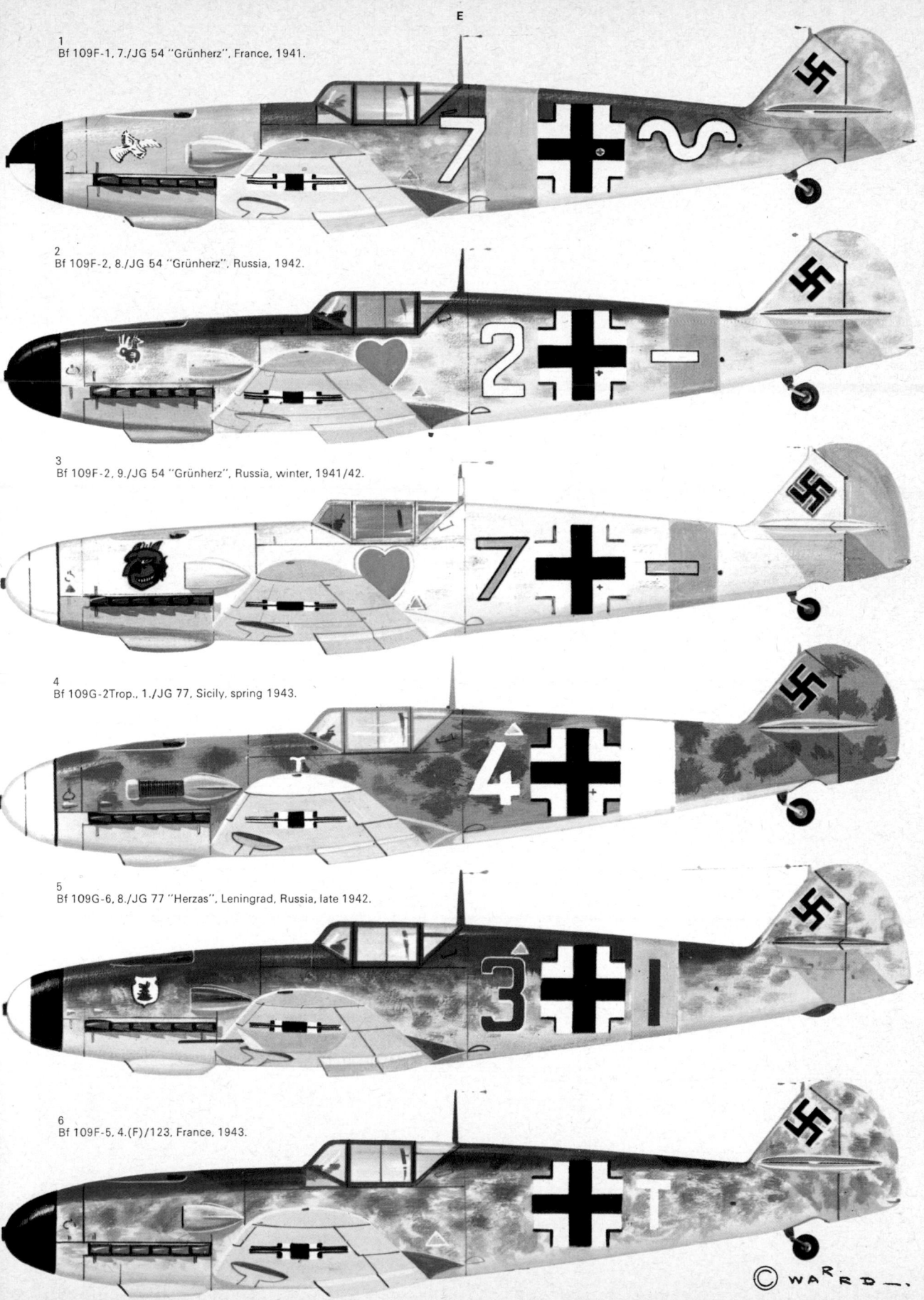

1
Bf 109F-1, 7./JG 54 "Grünherz", France, 1941.

2
Bf 109F-2, 8./JG 54 "Grünherz", Russia, 1942.

3
Bf 109F-2, 9./JG 54 "Grünherz", Russia, winter, 1941/42.

4
Bf 109G-2Trop., 1./JG 77, Sicily, spring 1943.

5
Bf 109G-6, 8./JG 77 "Herzas", Leningrad, Russia, late 1942.

6
Bf 109F-5, 4.(F)/123, France, 1943.

© WARD

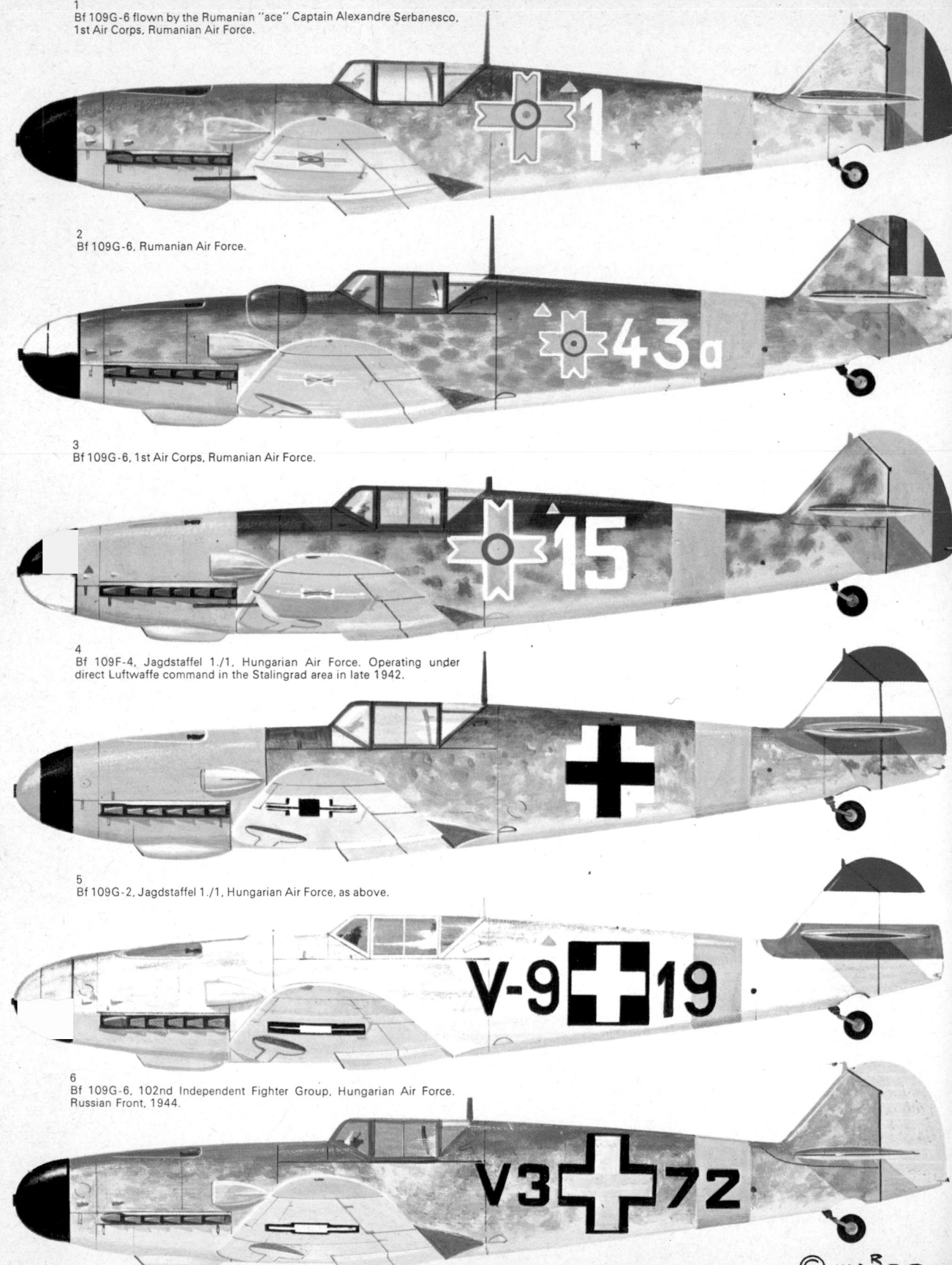

F

1
Bf 109G-6 flown by the Rumanian "ace" Captain Alexandre Serbanesco, 1st Air Corps, Rumanian Air Force.

2
Bf 109G-6, Rumanian Air Force.

3
Bf 109G-6, 1st Air Corps, Rumanian Air Force.

4
Bf 109F-4, Jagdstaffel 1./1, Hungarian Air Force. Operating under direct Luftwaffe command in the Stalingrad area in late 1942.

5
Bf 109G-2, Jagdstaffel 1./1, Hungarian Air Force, as above.

6
Bf 109G-6, 102nd Independent Fighter Group, Hungarian Air Force. Russian Front, 1944.

© WARD

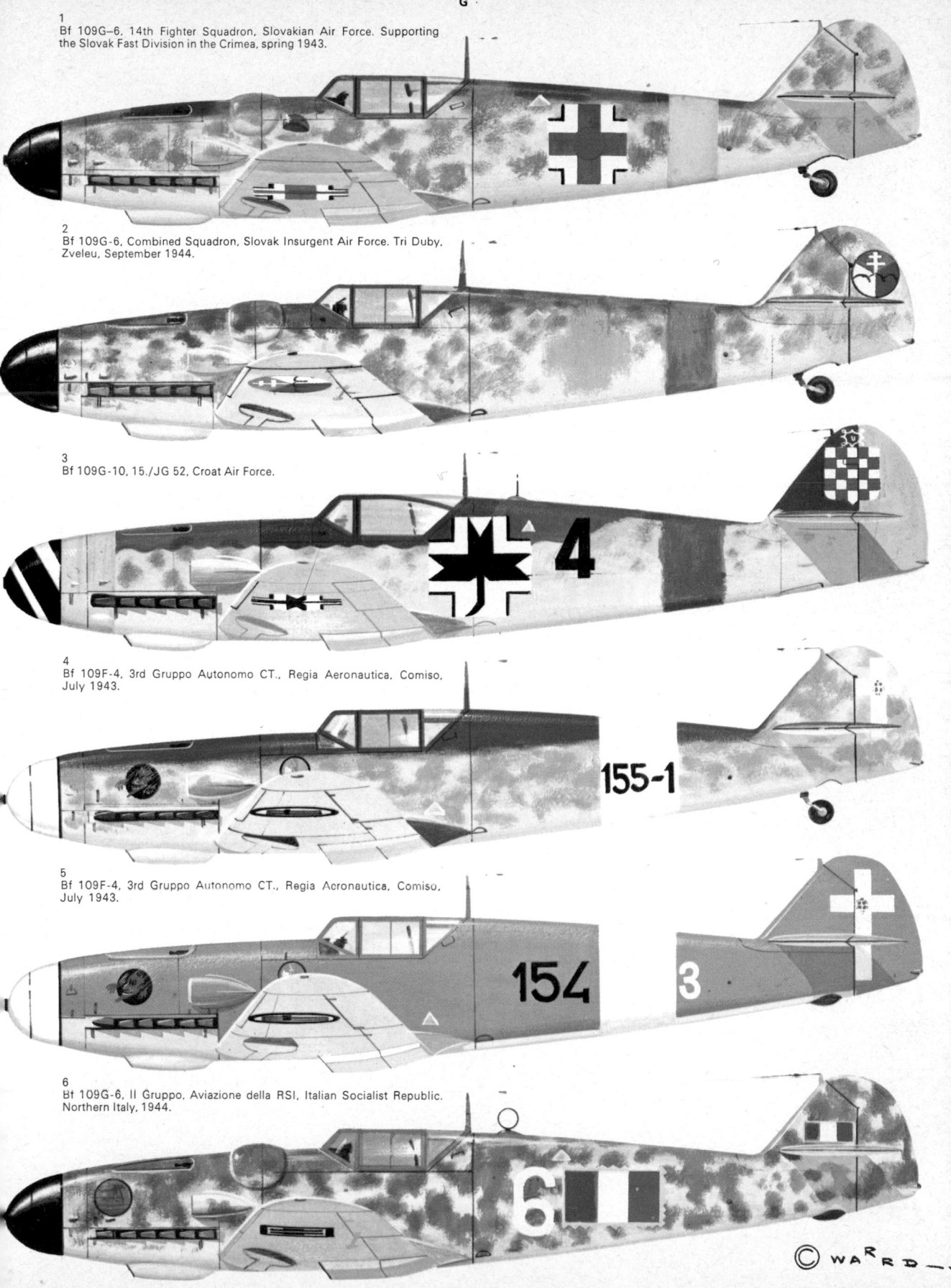

G

1
Bf 109G–6, 14th Fighter Squadron, Slovakian Air Force. Supporting the Slovak Fast Division in the Crimea, spring 1943.

2
Bf 109G-6, Combined Squadron, Slovak Insurgent Air Force. Tri Duby, Zveleu, September 1944.

3
Bf 109G-10, 15./JG 52, Croat Air Force.

4
Bf 109F-4, 3rd Gruppo Autonomo CT., Regia Aeronautica, Comiso, July 1943.

5
Bf 109F-4, 3rd Gruppo Autonomo CT., Regia Aeronautica, Comiso, July 1943.

6
Bf 109G-6, II Gruppo, Aviazione della RSI, Italian Socialist Republic. Northern Italy, 1944.

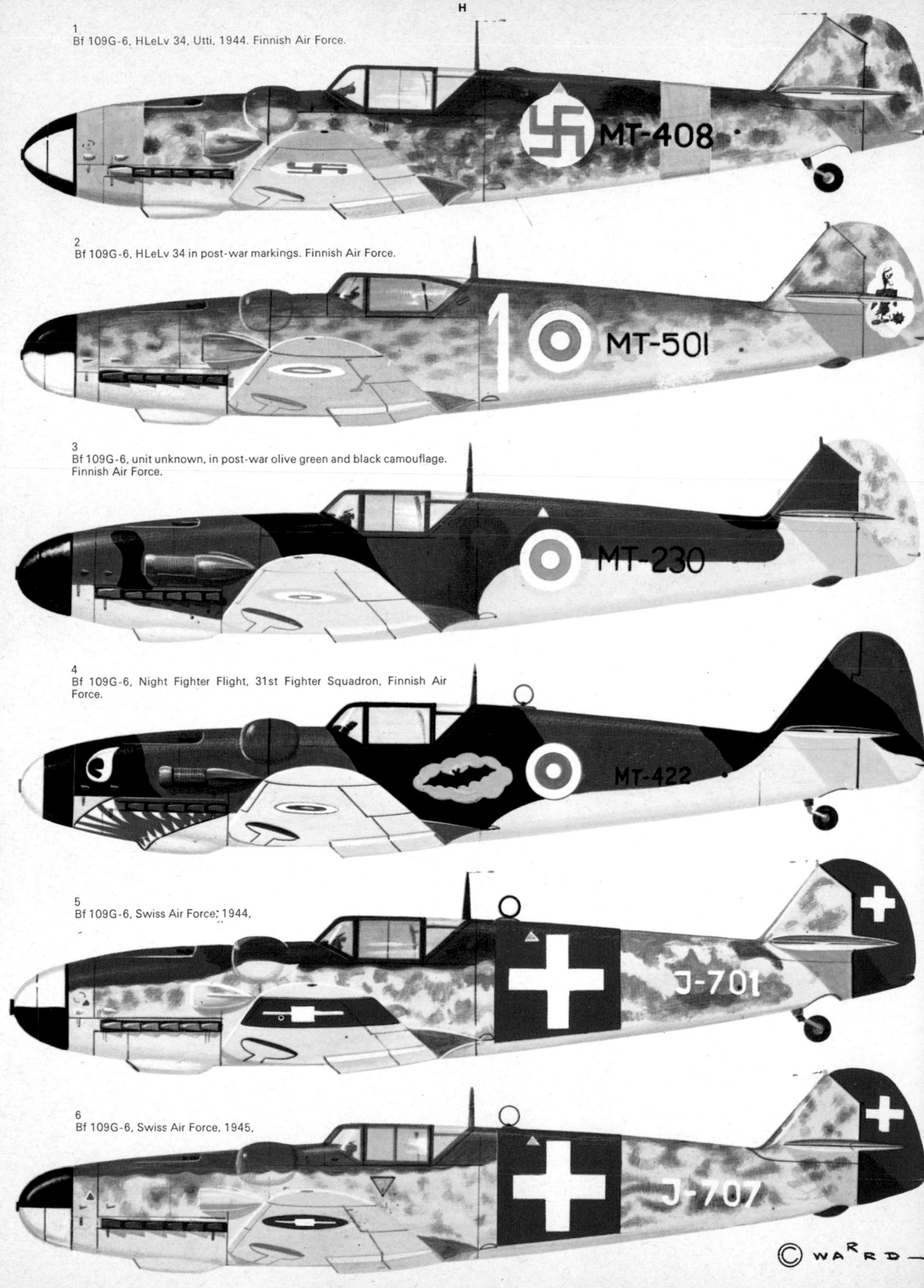

1
Bf 109G-6, HLeLv 34, Utti, 1944. Finnish Air Force.

2
Bf 109G-6, HLeLv 34 in post-war markings. Finnish Air Force.

3
Bf 109G-6, unit unknown, in post-war olive green and black camouflage. Finnish Air Force.

4
Bf 109G-6, Night Fighter Flight, 31st Fighter Squadron, Finnish Air Force.

5
Bf 109G-6, Swiss Air Force, 1944.

6
Bf 109G-6, Swiss Air Force, 1945.

© WARD

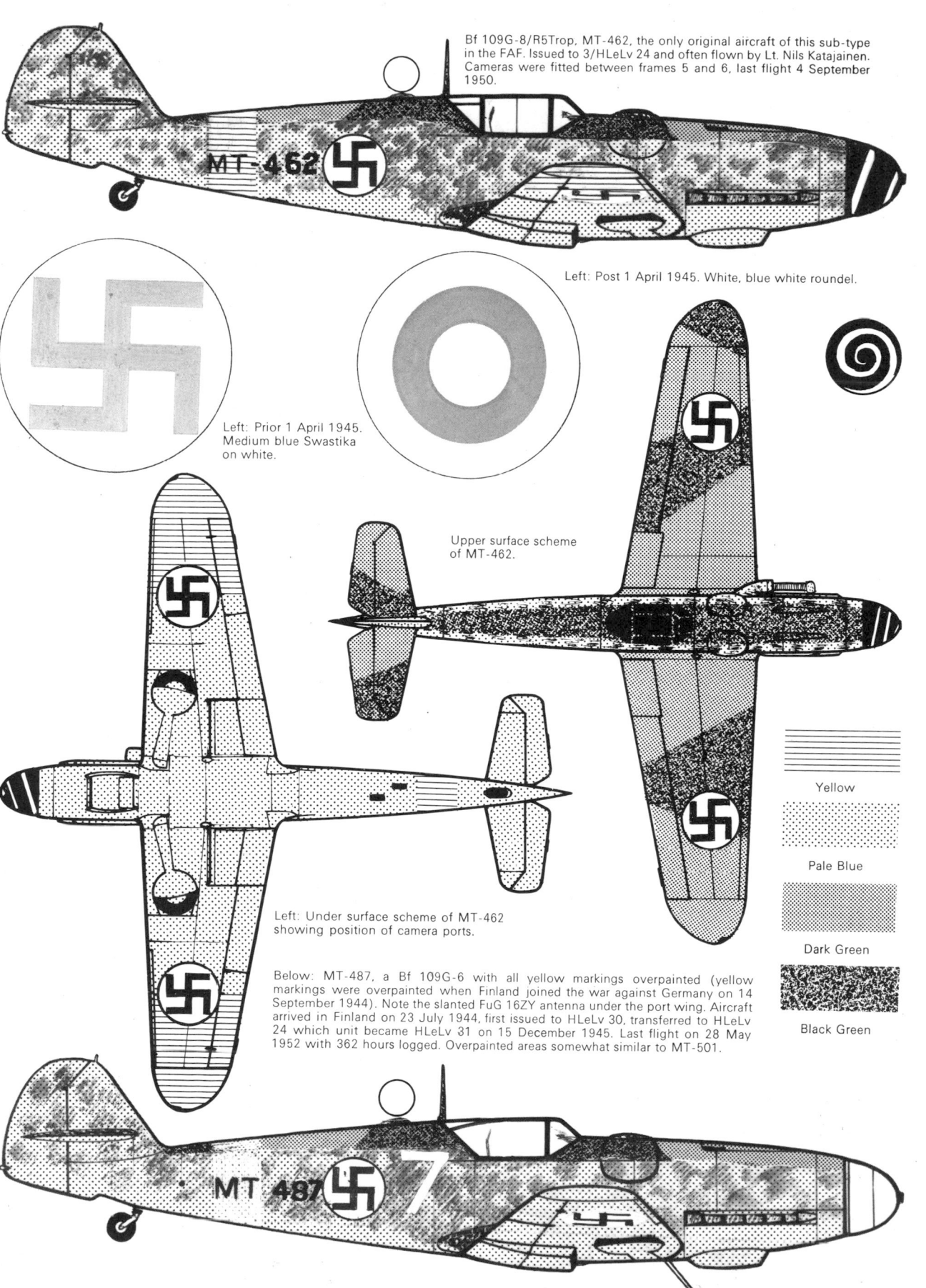

Bf 109G-8/R5Trop, MT-462, the only original aircraft of this sub-type in the FAF. Issued to 3/HLeLv 24 and often flown by Lt. Nils Katajainen. Cameras were fitted between frames 5 and 6, last flight 4 September 1950.

Left: Post 1 April 1945. White, blue white roundel.

Left: Prior 1 April 1945. Medium blue Swastika on white.

Upper surface scheme of MT-462.

Left: Under surface scheme of MT-462 showing position of camera ports.

Below: MT-487, a Bf 109G-6 with all yellow markings overpainted (yellow markings were overpainted when Finland joined the war against Germany on 14 September 1944). Note the slanted FuG 16ZY antenna under the port wing. Aircraft arrived in Finland on 23 July 1944, first issued to HLeLv 30, transferred to HLeLv 24 which unit became HLeLv 31 on 15 December 1945. Last flight on 28 May 1952 with 362 hours logged. Overpainted areas somewhat similar to MT-501.

Yellow

Pale Blue

Dark Green

Black Green

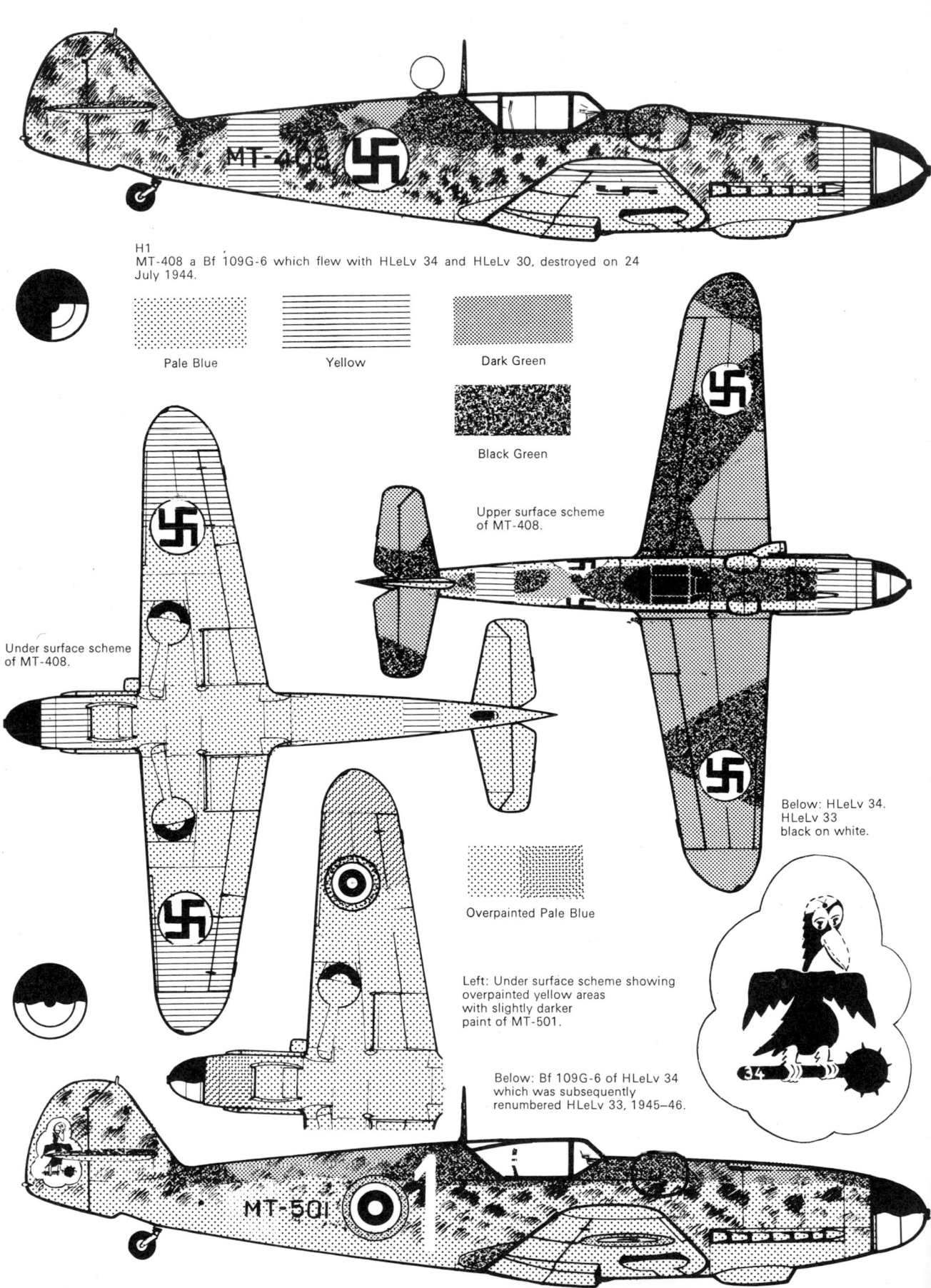

H1
MT-408 a Bf 109G-6 which flew with HLeLv 34 and HLeLv 30, destroyed on 24 July 1944.

Pale Blue

Yellow

Dark Green

Black Green

Upper surface scheme of MT-408.

Under surface scheme of MT-408.

Overpainted Pale Blue

Below: HLeLv 34. HLeLv 33 black on white.

Left: Under surface scheme showing overpainted yellow areas with slightly darker paint of MT-501.

Below: Bf 109G-6 of HLeLv 34 which was subsequently renumbered HLeLv 33, 1945–46.

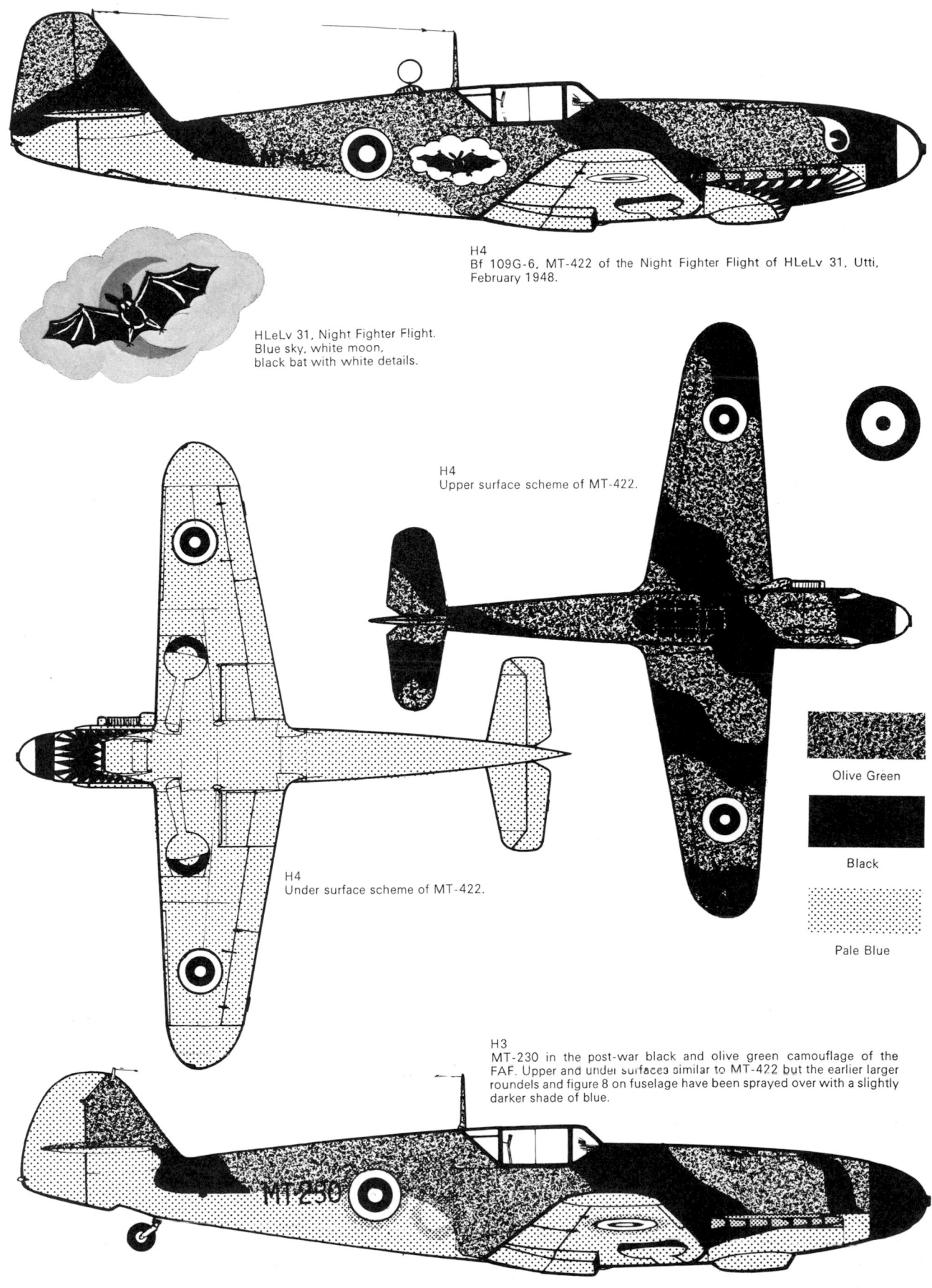

H4
Bf 109G-6, MT-422 of the Night Fighter Flight of HLeLv 31, Utti, February 1948.

HLeLv 31, Night Fighter Flight. Blue sky, white moon, black bat with white details.

H4
Upper surface scheme of MT-422.

H4
Under surface scheme of MT-422.

Olive Green

Black

Pale Blue

H3
MT-230 in the post-war black and olive green camouflage of the FAF. Upper and under surfaces similar to MT-422 but the earlier larger roundels and figure 8 on fuselage have been sprayed over with a slightly darker shade of blue.

Above: MT-426 a Bf 109G-6 probably of HLeLv 34 flying over Taipalsaari during the summer of 1944 in full yellow markings and with white 5 ahead of cockpit. (K. Toumikoski via Borje Hielm)

Right: A pair of Bf 109G-2s of HLeLv 34 during 1943, nearest aircraft is MT-229 the other MT-218. (via Eino Ritaranta)

Right: MT-501 a Bf 109G-6 of HLeLv 33 during late 1945.

Below: The black and white crow insignia of HLeLv 34 photographed at Taipalsaari during the summer of 1944; left and right is the insignia of HLeLv 33 at a later date. Note the differences. (via Borje Hielm)

Above: With black and white spiral spinner M I -503 a Bf 109G-6 of HLeLv 33 taxis out for take-off from Utti during the summer of 1947. (via Borje Hielm)

Above: MT-504 of HLeLv 31 photographed during 1948. Black spinner, Galland hood and FuG 16ZY aerial under port wing, white 6 ahead of cockpit.
(via Borje Hielm)

Below: MT-230 in the olive green and black camouflage, unit unknown, probably HLeLv 31. Note the darker areas where the earlier larger insignia has been overpainted. (via Eino Ritaranta)

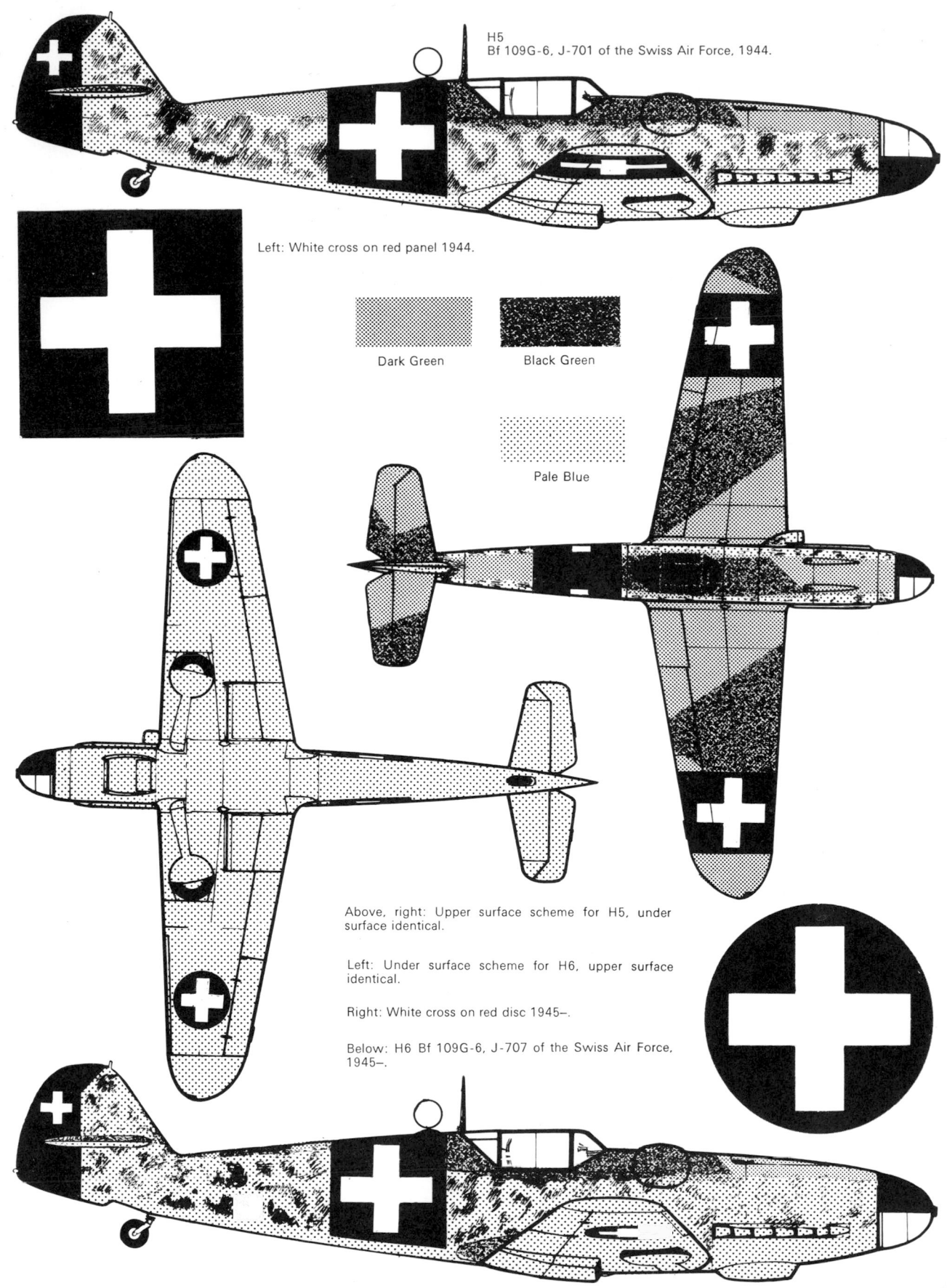

H5
Bf 109G-6, J-701 of the Swiss Air Force, 1944.

Left: White cross on red panel 1944.

Dark Green

Black Green

Pale Blue

Above, right: Upper surface scheme for H5, under surface identical.

Left: Under surface scheme for H6, upper surface identical.

Right: White cross on red disc 1945–.

Below: H6 Bf 109G-6, J-707 of the Swiss Air Force, 1945–.

Above: Bf 109G-6 of the 3rd Gruppo Autonomo on a Sicilian airfield. (Italian Air Force via C. F. Shores)

Left: Close-up of the 3rd Gruppo insignia, earlier the 6th Gruppo, "Diavoli Rossi". (IWM)

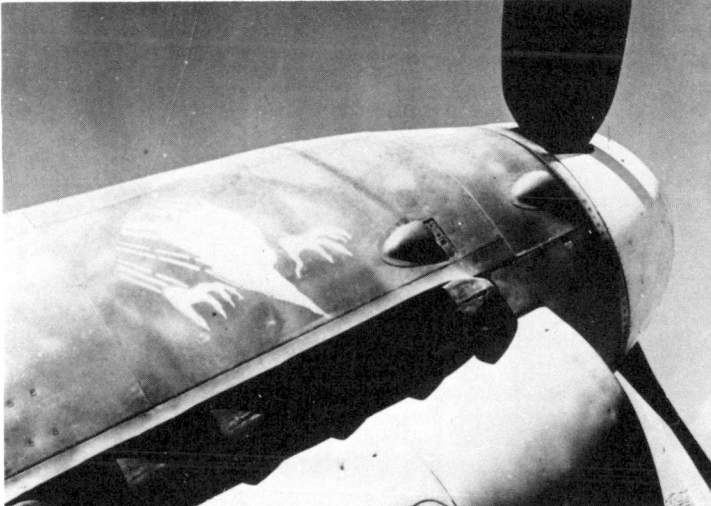

Below: Bf 109G-6 of the II Gruppo Aviazione della RSI, starboard side identical, standard Luftwaffe scheme with very heavy dark green dapple on fuselage.

Below: Bf 109G-6s of the II Gruppo, RSI taking off from a Northern Italian airfield in 1944. (G. Cattaneo)

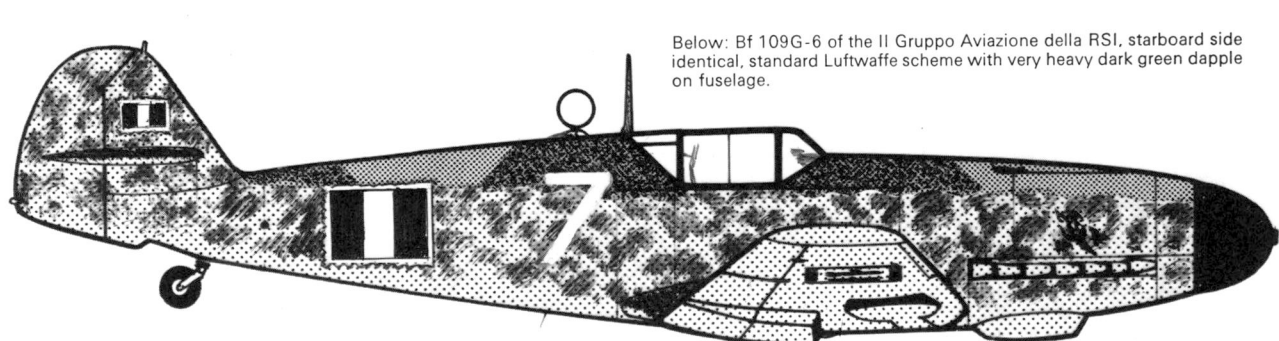

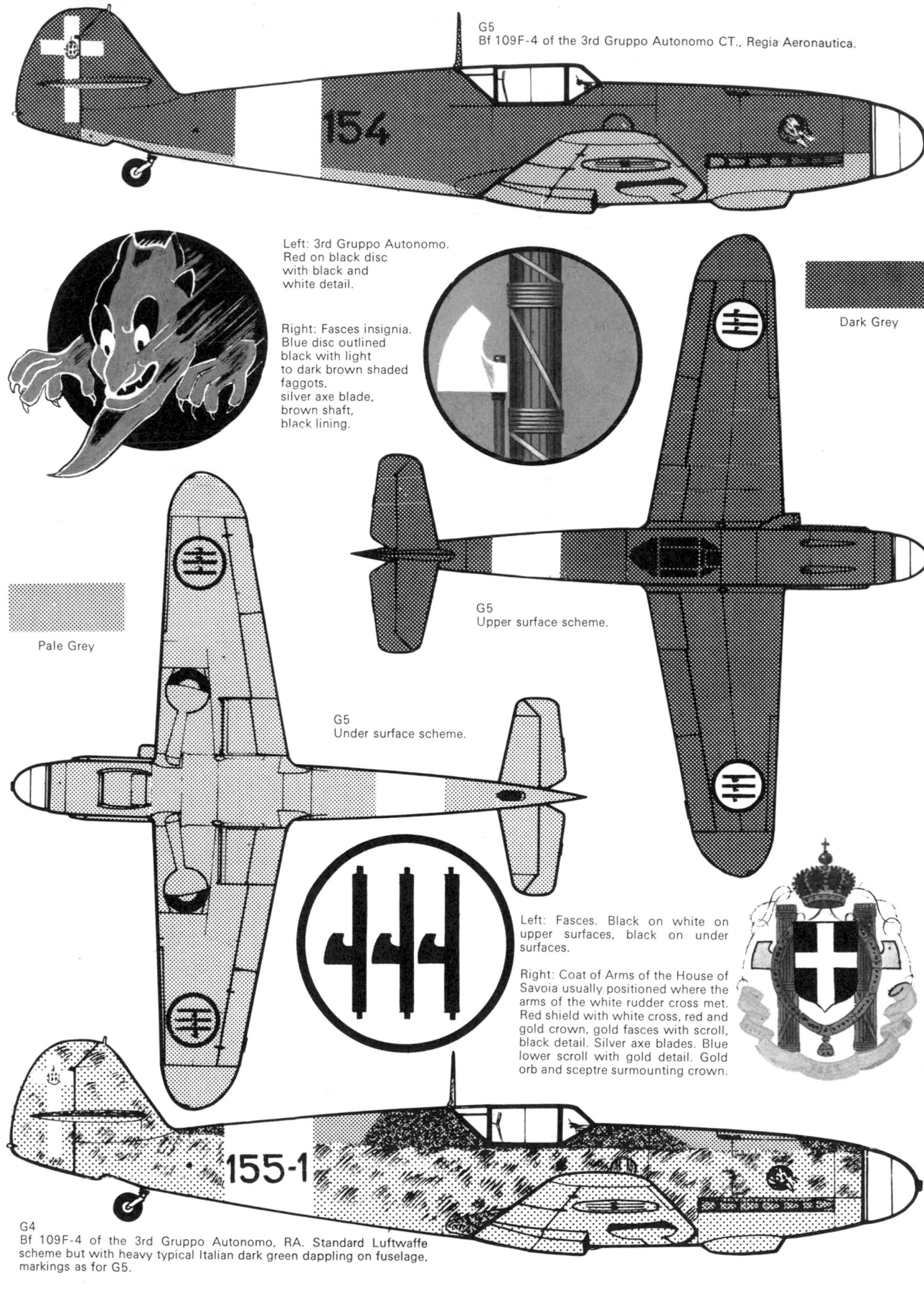

G5
Bf 109F-4 of the 3rd Gruppo Autonomo CT., Regia Aeronautica.

154

Left: 3rd Gruppo Autonomo. Red on black disc with black and white detail.

Right: Fasces insignia. Blue disc outlined black with light to dark brown shaded faggots, silver axe blade, brown shaft, black lining.

Dark Grey

Pale Grey

G5
Upper surface scheme.

G5
Under surface scheme.

Left: Fasces. Black on white on upper surfaces, black on under surfaces.

Right: Coat of Arms of the House of Savoia usually positioned where the arms of the white rudder cross met. Red shield with white cross, red and gold crown, gold fasces with scroll, black detail. Silver axe blades. Blue lower scroll with gold detail. Gold orb and sceptre surmounting crown.

155-1

G4
Bf 109F-4 of the 3rd Gruppo Autonomo, RA. Standard Luftwaffe scheme but with heavy typical Italian dark green dappling on fuselage, markings as for G5.

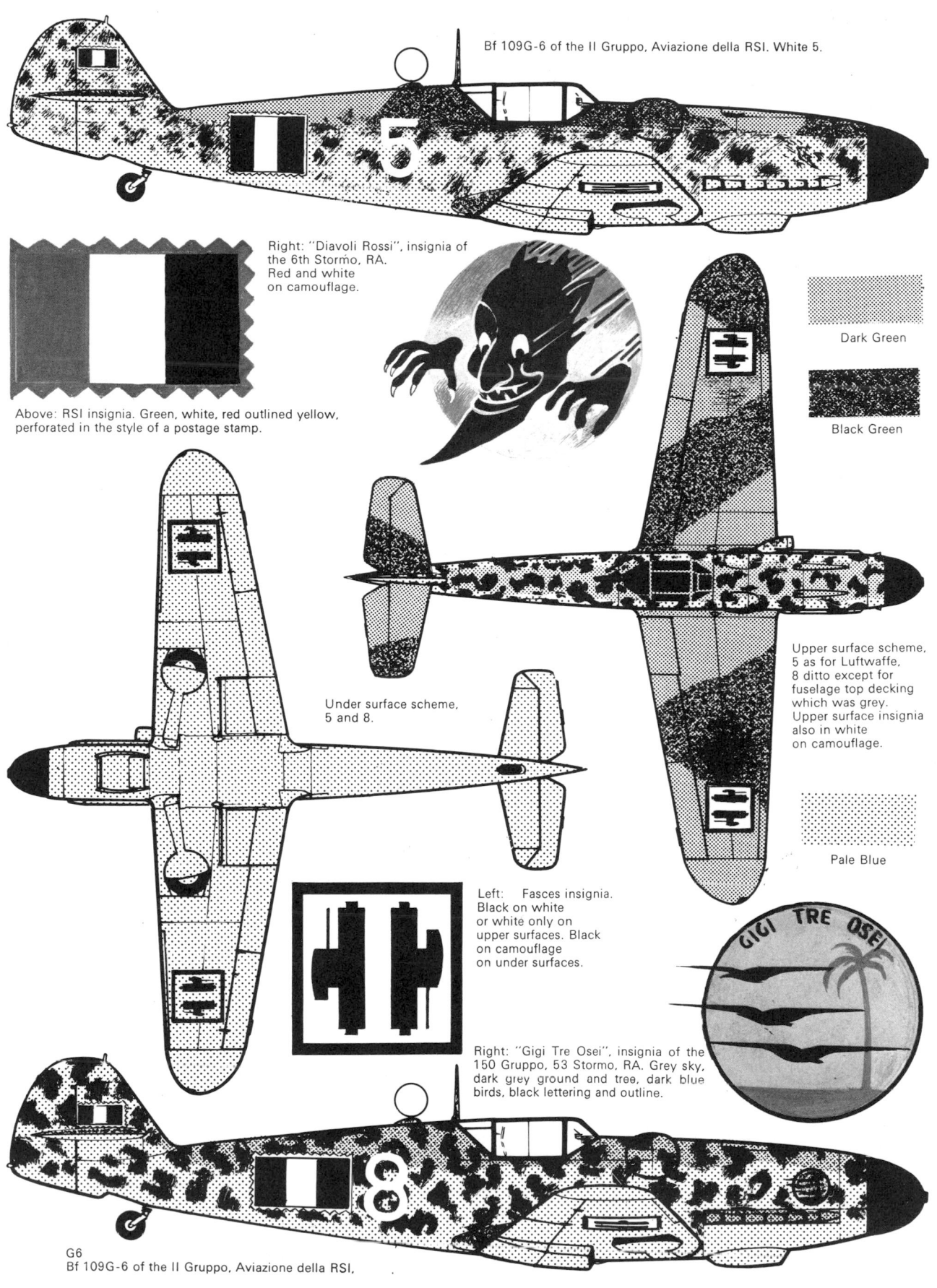

Bf 109G-6 of the II Gruppo, Aviazione della RSI. White 5.

Right: "Diavoli Rossi", insignia of the 6th Stormo, RA. Red and white on camouflage.

Above: RSI insignia. Green, white, red outlined yellow, perforated in the style of a postage stamp.

Dark Green

Black Green

Under surface scheme, 5 and 8.

Upper surface scheme, 5 as for Luftwaffe, 8 ditto except for fuselage top decking which was grey. Upper surface insignia also in white on camouflage.

Pale Blue

Left: Fasces insignia. Black on white or white only on upper surfaces. Black on camouflage on under surfaces.

Right: "Gigi Tre Osei", insignia of the 150 Gruppo, 53 Stormo, RA. Grey sky, dark grey ground and tree, dark blue birds, black lettering and outline.

GIGI TRE OSEI

G6
Bf 109G-6 of the II Gruppo, Aviazione della RSI,

A Hungarian Air Force Bf 109G-6 on a Me 262 in a post-war graveyard.

Bf 109G-1Trop of the Hungarian Air Force, 102/2 Fighter Squadron.

Left: Bf 109G-6 of the Rumanian Air Force. (Moisescu Mihail)

Below: With engine warming up a Rumanian Air Force Bf 109G-6 awaits the take-off signal. White 31. (Moisescu Mihail)

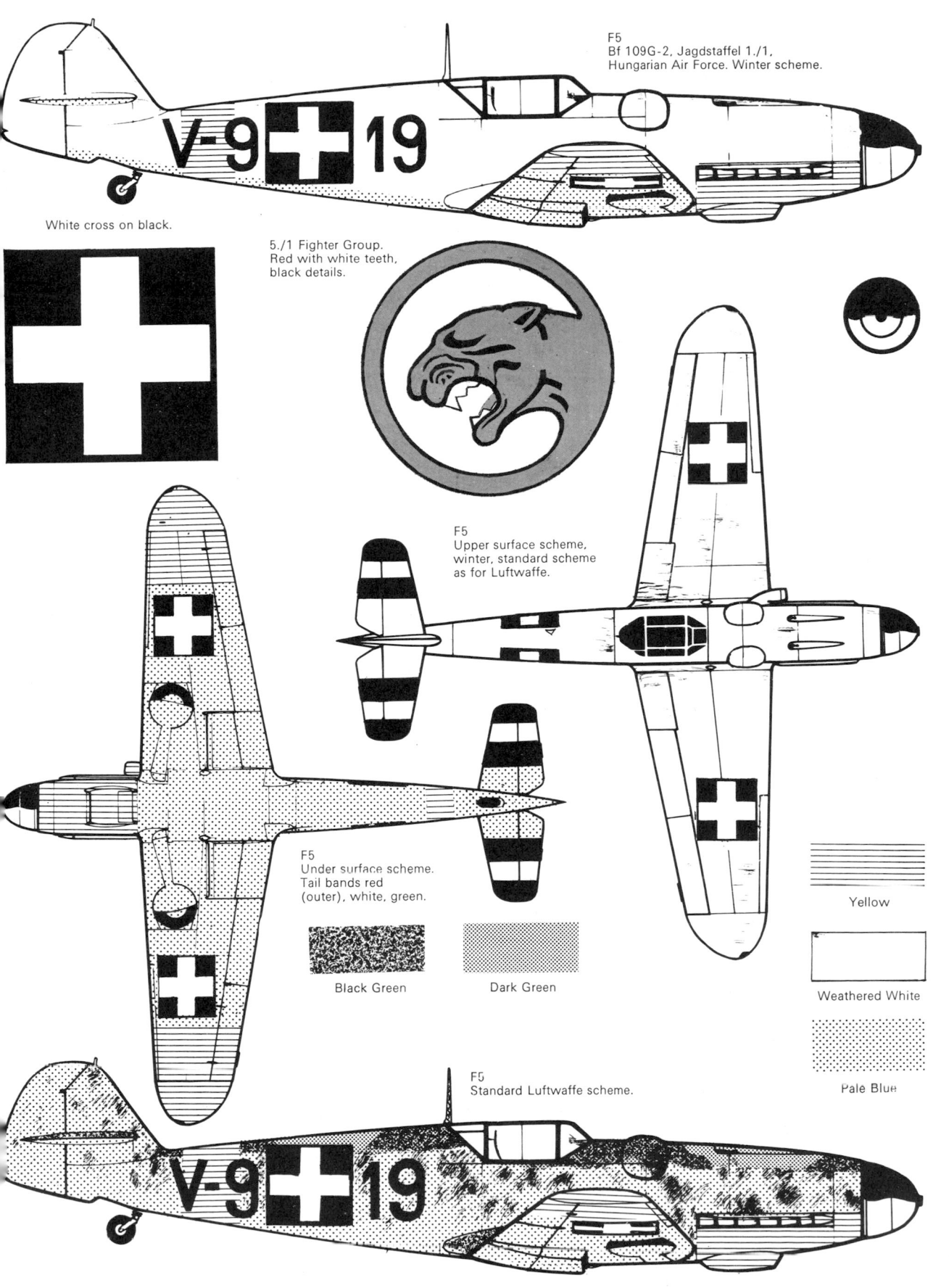

F5
Bf 109G-2, Jagdstaffel 1./1,
Hungarian Air Force. Winter scheme.

White cross on black.

5./1 Fighter Group.
Red with white teeth,
black details.

F5
Upper surface scheme,
winter, standard scheme
as for Luftwaffe.

F5
Under surface scheme.
Tail bands red
(outer), white, green.

Black Green

Dark Green

F5
Standard Luftwaffe scheme.

Yellow

Weathered White

Pale Blue

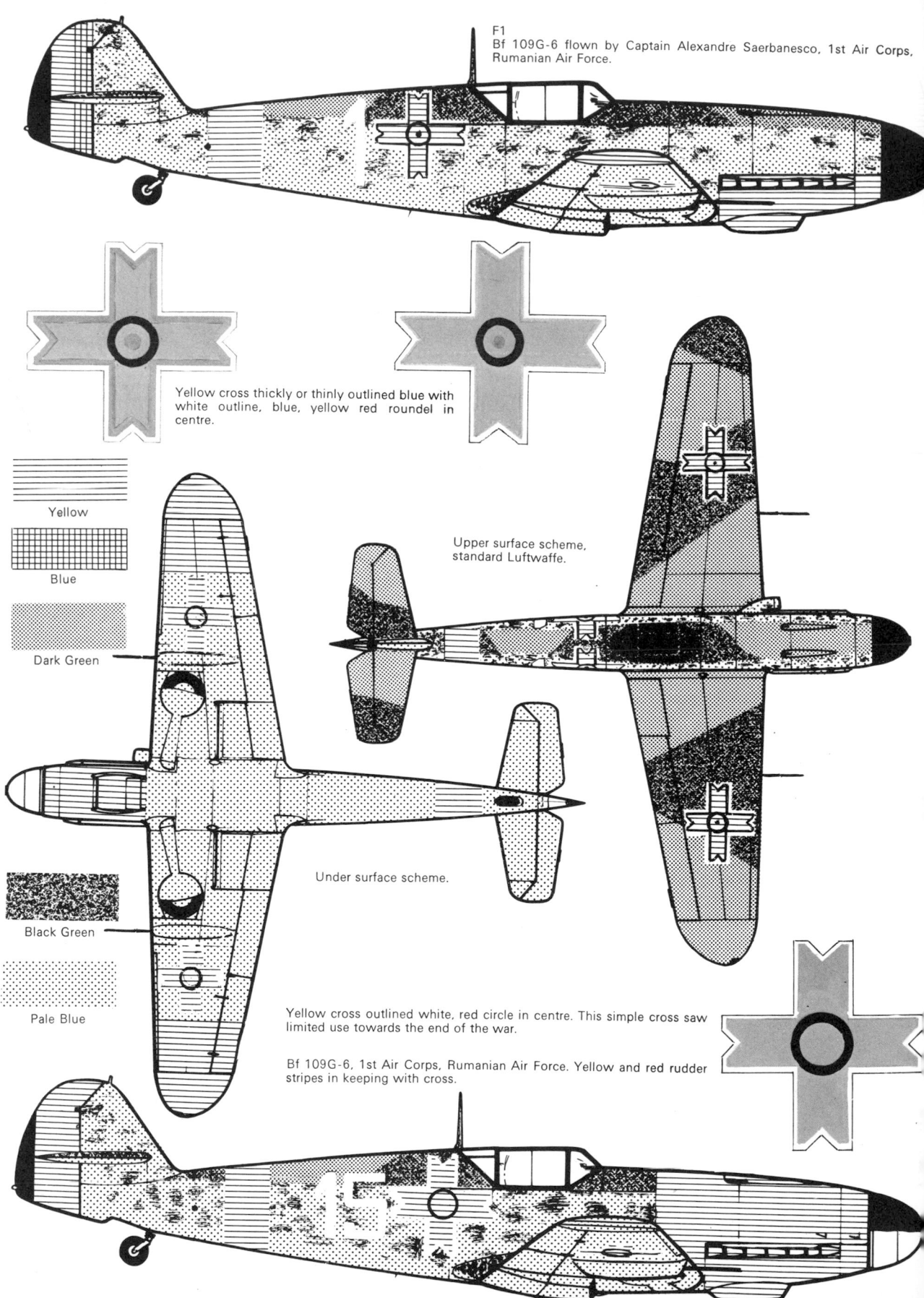

F1
Bf 109G-6 flown by Captain Alexandre Saerbanesco, 1st Air Corps, Rumanian Air Force.

Yellow cross thickly or thinly outlined blue with white outline, blue, yellow red roundel in centre.

Yellow

Blue

Dark Green

Upper surface scheme, standard Luftwaffe.

Black Green

Pale Blue

Under surface scheme.

Yellow cross outlined white, red circle in centre. This simple cross saw limited use towards the end of the war.

Bf 109G-6, 1st Air Corps, Rumanian Air Force. Yellow and red rudder stripes in keeping with cross.

G3
Bf 109G-10, 15./JG 52, Croat Air Force.

Ustachi insignia.
Red and white checks.

Cross of King Zvonomir.
Black and white.

Upper surface scheme,
standard Luftwaffe.

Under surface scheme.

Yellow

Dark Green

Black Green

Pale Blue

15./JG 52 Croat Staffel. Red and white with
black lining, grey wings.

TP2
Bf 109G-2, 15./JG 52, Croat Air Force operating
under direct Luftwaffe command.

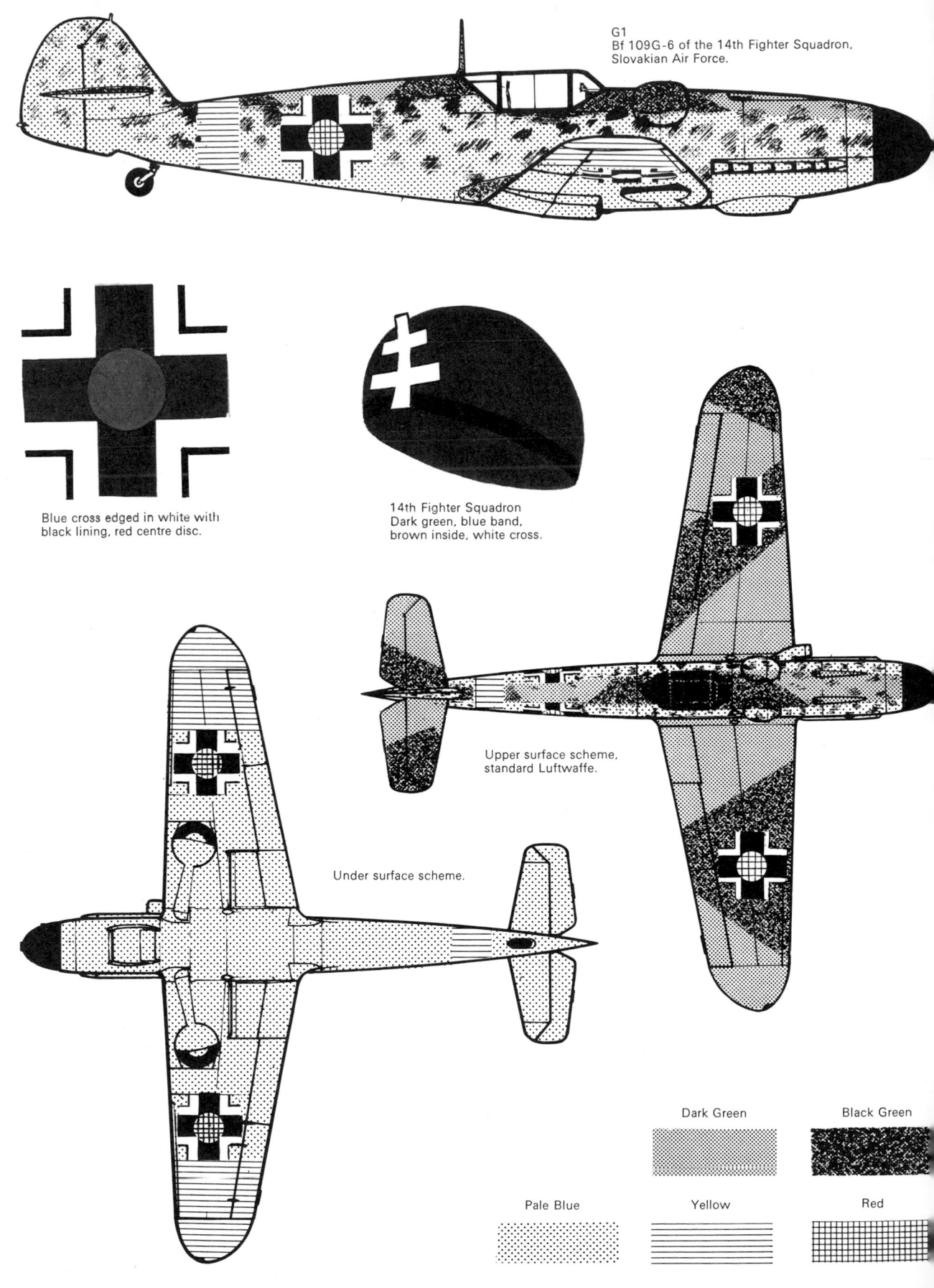

G1
Bf 109G-6 of the 14th Fighter Squadron,
Slovakian Air Force.

Blue cross edged in white with
black lining, red centre disc.

14th Fighter Squadron
Dark green, blue band,
brown inside, white cross.

Upper surface scheme,
standard Luftwaffe.

Under surface scheme.

Dark Green

Black Green

Pale Blue

Yellow

Red

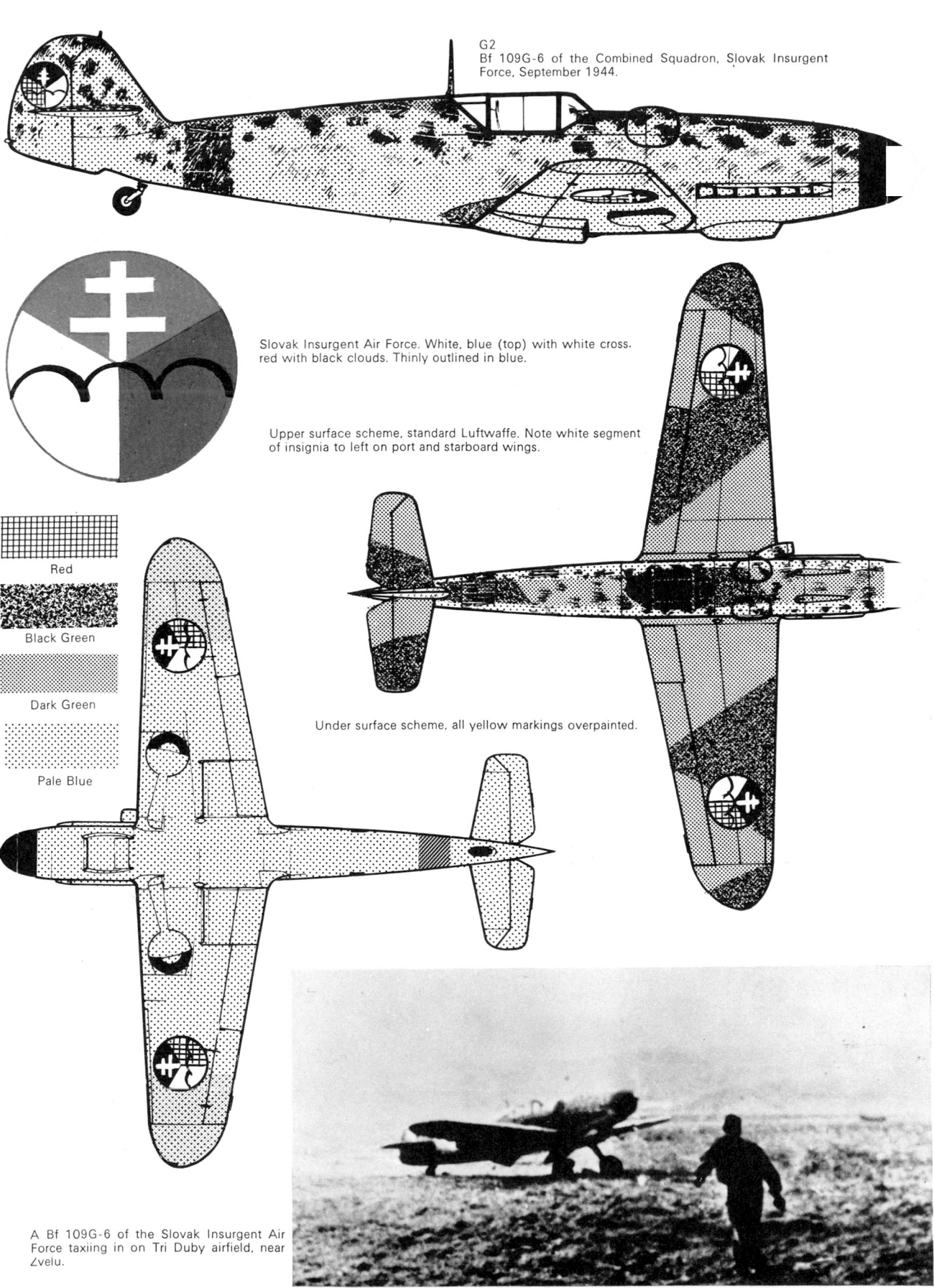

G2
Bf 109G-6 of the Combined Squadron, Slovak Insurgent Force, September 1944.

Slovak Insurgent Air Force. White, blue (top) with white cross, red with black clouds. Thinly outlined in blue.

Upper surface scheme, standard Luftwaffe. Note white segment of insignia to left on port and starboard wings.

Red

Black Green

Dark Green

Pale Blue

Under surface scheme, all yellow markings overpainted.

A Bf 109G-6 of the Slovak Insurgent Air Force taxiing in on Tri Duby airfield, near Zvelu.

Above: A Bf 109G-10 of 15./JG 52, the Croatian Staffel surrendered by its pilot to US Forces at Falconara in Italy, April 1945. (USAF)

Left: Bf 109G-14, Avia C-10 of the Czechoslovak Air Force. (Z. Titz)

Left & below: Bf 109G-12 trainer, Avia C-110 in overall silver scheme, airscrew tips are yellow black yellow. (Z Titz)